Finding Your Voice

Laura G. Manis and Lisa Neela Manis

Finding Your Voice

Self-Esteem and Assertiveness Training for Teen Girls

- by not hurting others
- by learning social skills
- by saying what you mean
- by standing up for yourself
- by being responsible for your actions

A Leader's Guide for a Training Workshop

Laura G. Manis and Lisa Neela Manis

Learning Publications, Inc.
Holmes Beach, Florida

ISBN 1-55691-222-6

© 2001 by Laura G. Manis and Lisa Neela Manis

All rights reserved. No part of this book may be reproduced or transmitted in any form or by any means, electronic or mechanical, including photocopying and recording, or by any information or retrieval systems, without permission in writing from the publisher.

Learning Publications, Inc.
5351 Gulf Drive
P.O. Box 1338
Holmes Beach, FL 34218-1338

Printing: 5 4 3 2 1   Year: 05 04 03 02 01

Illustrations by Alan Dulfon

Printed in the United States of America

Contents

Preface vii

Introduction xi

Workshop Overview xvii

Session 1: What is Assertive Behavior 1

Overview • Presession Self-Assessment • What Is This Workshop About? • Introductions • Getting from Here to There • Do You Like String Beans? • Keeping Confidences • What is Assertive Behavior? • Your Body Talks Too • Telling the Difference • Finding Your Comfort Level • Closing the Session • The Link • Supplemental Instruction: The Name Game • Do I Have Trouble with Any of These?

Session 2: Identifying Feelings 25

Overview • Homework Review • Desensitization to Eye Contact • Listening and Hearing • Name that Feeling • What Do I Like to Do? • What Do I Like About Myself? • Giving and Receiving Compliments • Compliment Scramble • Closing the Session

Session 3: Values and Respecting Rights 41

Overview • Homework Review • My Values • Rights and Responsibilities • Other People's Rights • The Swap Meet • Rights Role Play • Closing the Session

Session 4: Blocks to Assertion 53

Overview • Homework Review • What This Session Is About • Stop That Thought! • Bad News Beliefs • Bad News, Good News • Stopping My Bad News Voice • Finding My Magnificent True Self • Closing the Session • Supplemental Instruction: Take a Deep Breath

Session 5: Learning to Say "No" 71

Overview • Homework Review • Peer Pressure • Handling Peer Pressure • Give Me Some Space • Refusing Requests • Role Playing Saying "No" • Combining Persistence with Understanding and a Workable Compromise • Closing the Session • Supplemental Exercise: Negotiating a Workable Compromise

Session 6: Mistakes, Criticism, Feelings, and Needs 87

Overview • Homework Review • Admitting Mistakes • Handling Criticism (Put-downs) • Expressing Feelings and Needs Assertively ("I" Language) • Keeping Cool to Critics (Diversion) • Closing the Session

Session 7: Social Skills.. 99

    Overview • Homework Review • Starting Conversations or the Game of Catch • Breaking Into Conversations • Behavior Rehearsal with Muscle • Aftereffects: Setting Goals • Post-session Self-Assessment • Closing the Session and Ending the Workshop • Skill Exercise: You're Awesome!

Appendix A: Resource Sheets..111

Appendix B: What to Say When Problems Pop Up – Some Typical Challenges.....................205

Appendix C: Games..207

Appendix D: Suggested Agenda for a One-Day Introductory Workshop 209

Appendix E: Glossary 211

Appendix F: Journal of Assertive Behavior...213

Appendix G: Resources and Recommended Reading..215

Preface

When I was suffering through the throes of adolescence, struck dumb with shyness, feeling too tall, too skinny, feeling different, awkward, unattractive, I was always told "just be yourself." But that was the problem! I didn't know what that was.

Now, with the hindsight of years, I realize that not being able to articulate what I felt, what I thought, or what I needed was at the root of my sometimes antisocial behavior. It also resulted in problems with my parents, my hurt feelings, my low self-esteem, and my vulnerability to being swayed by my friends.

This manual is an attempt to give girls from about the ages of 12 to 17 some tools that will help them through those turbulent years with greater assurance and lessened fear while they clarify who they are.

My experience developing and facilitating programs for women of all ages has taught me that assertion training is a basic skill that can be taught and that it increases self-esteem which in turn provides the strength to change behavior.

Times have changed since I was an adolescent. Thirty-eight percent of women who have been raped were 14–17 years old at the time of the attack, most by a date or a friend. Over three million Americans age 14–17, are considered problem drinkers, 50 percent of teen pregnancies are alcohol related. According to Simon and Harris, *Sex Without Consent,* those students who have initiated or engaged in nonconsensual sexual activity may have inadequate assertiveness, decision-making, and communication skills.

The pressures on teenagers are different but the tools to help cope with the pressures have been tested and they work.

Laura G. Manis

Acknowledgments

We would like to thank several people who contributed their thoughts, ideas, and counsel. Anni Lindenberg, Meredith Madden, our teen-age consultants who allowed us to practice on them, gave us their thoughts, revealed their feelings, and told us their needs. The folks at Hale Kipa, Honolulu, a shelter for teenage runaways explained the extent and ramifications of the problem of low self-esteem and Dr. Meda Chesney Lind a sociologist at the University of Hawaii who pointed to research statistics, and references explaining the world of the adolescent girl.

A special thanks to Learning Publications and Edsel Erickson, who encouraged us to write this manual and supported our efforts.

The pleasure of a family joint project was increased by the support and patience of Jerome Manis, husband and father. Thanks for letting me hog the computer!

Finally, a number of the activities have come to us from other teachers, counselors, and group leaders. It has been difficult and sometimes impossible to identify the original source. Wherever possible, we have done our best to give the appropriate credit.

Introduction

Finding Your Voice has been developed around the particular characteristics of young adolescent girls. The exercises have been chosen with these traits in mind. What are these traits? What social, physical, and emotional problems can these traits create? How do they affect a girl's self-esteem? And how does learning assertive skills enhance self-esteem and so make it more likely that many of the problems of adolescence can be handled more adequately.

Following is a chart that illustrates the answers to the above questions and how the exercises in this manual and its general perspective relate to each other.

Traits	Challenges	Change Techniques
Sexual development	Sexual harassment, abuse, pregnancy, sexually transmitted disease	Learning rights, how to say no, refuse requests, gaining self-respect
Self-conscious, hypersensitive, self-critical	Low self-esteem, shyness or extroversion, anorexia, need for privacy	Social-skill exercises, role-playing practice, positive feedback in safe environment, self-appreciation, support
Prefer active over passive learning	Fidgety, restless	All sessions include interactive exercises
Idealistic, emotional	Argumentative, difficulties with parents, searching for answers/justice	Practice in dealing with criticism, anger, expressing feelings, communication skills, expressing and defending opinions
Peer group most important, intolerant of differences, egocentric, curious	Irresponsible behavior, no consideration of consequences, feelings of rejection, need to be like everyone else, pressure to experiment with drugs, sex, alcohol	Resisting peer pressure, feedback from group members, admitting mistakes, considering consequences, considering rights of others, relieving stress
Rejection of adult standards and social values	Testing limits, questioning values, vulnerability to naive arguments	Listening skills, empathy, value clarification
Basic optimism, emerging sense of humor	Relationships, school	Humor vs. sarcasm, considering consequences
Desires independence but wants boundaries	Conflicts with parents, awkward with authority figures	Expressing needs, learning and practicing empathy, negotiating

Self-Esteem and Assertive Behavior

The primary goal of assertive behavior is to increase self-esteem. What is self-esteem and what is the relationship between self-esteem and how we manage life's challenges? And how does learning assertive skills help to increase self-esteem?

Self-esteem means valuing yourself. It comes from the thoughts, feelings, and experiences one has and will have throughout life. Assertive behavior is being able to stand up for yourself by expressing your thoughts, feelings and beliefs in direct, honest, and appropriate ways that do not violate the rights of others. Acting in such a way leads to high self-esteem and learning this skill provides the tools to use in achieving high self-esteem.

To advance that goal, this book presents direct, uncomplicated, nonthreatening exercises progressing from simple to more complex situations.

Lack of assertiveness undermines self-worth and increases negative self-judgments, and decreases the likelihood of exhibiting more positive behaviors that would increase self-esteem.

When adolescents display poor social skills and low self-esteem, the process of regaining the self-confidence to change behavior and attitudes takes time. But providing the opportunity to practice the new behavior in a safe environment and experiencing how good it feels and how it affects others, is a positive life-enhancing experience. Treating the cause rather than treating the symptoms, which is usually only a temporary relief, is much more effective. Significantly, R. Reasoner 1992, using a controlled study in three school districts, found that a structured program in self-esteem training considerably reduced the incidence of antisocial behavior in schools.

Clues to Low Self-Esteem

Girls can show low self-esteem in many ways, sometimes without even being aware that they don't feel good about themselves. Usually though, they have this vague feeling that something is wrong.

Here are some usual clues:

- whining
- perfectionism
- too self-critical
- always agreeable
- avoiding new experiences
- having to win
- clowning
- withdrawn
- sarcastic
- dieting/anorexia
- cheating
- teasing
- blaming
- indecisive
- angry/explosive
- bragging
- complaining
- always apologetic
- too passive
- drinking/drugs

About This Book

Finding Your Voice describes a seven-session workshop, that meets for about two hours each week. Each session deals with a specific topic. Each unit provides information and activities that build upon the preceding one.

The book provides the group leader with structured exercises that encourage active, supportive, and constructive group dynamics. Each session begins with an outline and includes the goals, materials required, exercises, step-by step instructions, short readings, supplemental exercises, and simple homework. All activity sheets, readings, and handouts to be used by the participants as worksheets or stimulus for group discussions and activities are included in Appendices A, E, and F and may be reproduced. Copies of journal sheets are provided (Appendix F) where attempts at assertive behavior can be recorded easily.

Settings: The material can by used in different settings; classrooms, girl's clubs, Girl Scouts, youth groups, youth outreach or intervention programs, juvenile court programs, and church groups. Since time constraints are different in each setting, the material can be allocated to fit the time as long as the material is presented in the same sequence as written here. Suggested times are included in the instructions to help with planning. These are only suggestions since anything can come up in a discussion and the leader may not wish to stop at the given time.

Supplemental Activities: Girls of 12 years of age can be quite different from those of 17 in terms of experience and development and every group is different. Therefore we have included supplemental exercises at the end of each session. These are to provide the leaders with flexibility in choosing exercises that fit their groups. Some of the supplemental activities may be more suitable for younger or older girls than those in the regular session. Some can be done faster or you may wish to go more into depth with a certain concept and include them in addition to the one in the session. These exercises may fit your particular group better than the ones used in the main session. You be the judge.

Gender Specific: The program was developed specifically for young teen-age girls using successful strategies to help them cope with their new bodies, new expectations and new pressures. Why not include teen-age boys? Because girls of this age need and learn from their peers. It becomes their pre-eminent reference group. Boys are often the problem. Having boys in the same group at this stage changes the whole dynamics and makes it less likely for either gender to feel secure and be honest. While girls need to learn how to relate to boys and vice versa, the additional pressure is best dealt with, perhaps, in a subsequent workshop.

Sequence of Activities: Commercial situations, since they are the most common and involve strangers are generally easier. Behavior is already known and expected, such as, with sales clerks, etc. Although for many teenagers, these are still hurdles to overcome.

The exercises, therefore, are in sequence from the easier commercial situations to the more difficult relationships: friends, family, and authority figure situations, especially friends.

Most of the book will deal with relationship and peer pressures. Rules of behavior for social situations are somewhat less rigid and the concern for its impact on relationships especially at these ages, make assertion most difficult. The need to "fit in," to be like everyone else, have best friends, to be liked, and to belong can cause feelings of being an actor on stage performing what is expected instead of paying attention to how one really feels and what feels right. This can lead to regret, guilt, uncomfortable and even dangerous situations.

Situations involving family members and authority figures are also of concern and the source of much conflict. Most parents say their teenagers have no trouble saying no to just about everything!

Past history, learned behavior, old feelings, new concerns, and important relationships all have to be considered in changing behavior. This takes time and can't be done in a day.

Most new group members have difficulty thinking of the right word or phrases to use in their assertion exercises. The beginning exercises include practice using suggested wording. As participants grow in confidence, they will provide their own wording.

The simple talks, discussions, readings, exercises, and most important—role play—will provide the participants with the integration of conceptual understanding and actual practice of assertive behavior.

Importance of Role Play

Role playing fills the gap between reading about behavior change and actually trying the behavior and hearing how it affects others.

Role plays are especially important as a means of practicing new behavior in a safe environment and acquiring constructive suggestions on how to improve. Role plays promote confidence and incorporates the behavior into the participant's repertoire of responses so that a more effective response becomes almost automatic when the actual situation arises.

The benefits of role plays:

- They reveal the difference between thinking and doing.
- They make clear that assertion training is a skill that can be learned in the same way riding a bicycle is a skill.
- They show that the behavior is not only a product of personality but also of the situations in which persons find themselves.
- The use of feedback in role playing trains the participant to be sensitive to the feelings of others and teaches the importance feelings play in determining behavior.
- They help people become aware of behaviors that may be hurtful to others. For example, using wisecracks or sarcasm often hurts others.
- They permit training in the control of feelings. For example, repeatedly playing the role of older sister gives practice in not becoming annoyed by little sister's nagging.
- They develop compassion and understanding of other points of view.
- Practice makes perfect. Students will gain confidence in using the new behavior.

General Training Guidelines

While extensive group training is not required for group leaders in order to use the exercises in this book successfully, it is expected that group leaders will have had some experience in a group setting and with the age group *Finding Your Voice* is intended to reach. For those readers who may want to learn more about the group process, facilitating groups and the therapeutic process, we have included resources and recommended readings in Appendix G.

The following is a list of general training strategies that we have found have worked well.

- Partner with a co-leader whenever possible. Two pairs of eyes, ears and brains helps you keep on top of things. If you are relatively inexperienced, find an experienced co-leader. If you are leading the group alone, limit the size to no more than eight.

- Participants who are not assertive and have low self-esteem may become easily discouraged. Therefore provide frequent, sincere praise for those first tries at assertive behavior during behavioral rehearsals and role playing. Emphasize what is positive in their performance. Find an occasion in each session to praise what each person has done well, then select one or at most two behaviors to improve at any one time. Don't overwhelm.

- During early training phases, give concrete feedback to participants by helping them arrive at the exact word and actions they might use in particular situations. A good way to help them start is to ask, "What do you want to accomplish?" "What would you have liked to have said?"

- Learning to distinguish assertive from unassertive and aggressive behavior is crucial. Most importantly, leaders should be able to reflect such discrimination in their own behavior.

- *Finding Your Voice* has an educational format. It is not group psychotherapy. If a participant is experiencing intense personal anguish and finding it difficult to concentrate and hold their lives together, then this workshop is not the place to begin. The workshop is brief and does not permit in-depth work with individual participants. Instead, it is recommended that these persons start with one-to-one counseling, and if they desire, enroll in an assertiveness workshop later.

- Members have the right to refuse to participate in any activity or reject suggestions without giving reasons. However, if a group member chooses not to do as suggested by the group leader, she is expected to do so in a manner that does not interfere with the participation of the other members.

- Resistance can be handled by asking participants to rehearse their own ways of handling a situation, then to practice the suggested assertive way. Encourage them to listen to feedback from other members in their group and then choose whichever method is most satisfying.

- Participants should rehearse all homework during group sessions before trying them in actual situations.

- It is important that participants understand that changes in their behavior may affect their relationships with their families and friends and even with teachers. Girls that have allowed others to make their decisions for them, or have been willing to do almost anything that a friend demanded may find that these people may be displeased and even shocked by their new behavior. Therefore, we suggest that members inform the important people in their lives that they are learning to behave differently—assertively—and would like encouragement, patience, and supportive feedback while they are learning.

- Participants should not rehearse role plays with the same group members each time, by changing partners they will learn how to respond to a variety of personalities.
- Display leadership behavior that is characterized by assertion rather than aggression or nonassertion.
- Finally, laugh and enjoy yourself. These kids are lots of fun. They may never be so droll, illogical, outrageous, or hilarious again. Laugh with them, at yourself, at life. Take advantage and nurture their budding sense of humor.

Workshop Overview

Session	Main Focus	Exercises	Homework Readings	Homework Activities
1	Learning How to Identify Assertive Behavior	Introductions, Do You Like String Beans? Keeping Confidences, What Is Assertive Behavior? Finding Your Comfort Level, The Link, Supplemental: Name Game, Do You Have Trouble with Any of These	Lisa's story, Getting from Here to There, What is Assertive Behavior? Keeping a Diary Helps	Daily Journal of Assertive Behavior, Discrimination Quiz, Introduce Yourself to Three Strangers, Record Three Observations, and Three Accomplishments
2	Listening Skills, Identifying Feelings, Likes, and Strengths	Eye Contact, Listening and Hearing, Name that Feeling, What Do I Like?, What Do I Like About Myself?, Giving and Receiving Compliments, Compliment Scramble, Supplemental: All About Me, Deeper Listening	I Like Me, Listening and Hearing	Get to Your Point, Practice Listening Skills, Journal Keeping
3	Values and Respecting Rights	My Value, Rights and Responsibilities, Personal Rights, Others' Rights, Rights and Responsibilities, Swap Meet, Supplemental: Additional Values, Discovering Me, Building Confidence	Misfits?	Giving Compliments, Using Rights, Practicing Listening Skills, Journals
4	Blocks to Assertion	Stop that Thought!, Bad New Beliefs, Bad News, Good News, Stopping My Bad News Voice, Journey to Meet My Magnificent True Self Supplemental: Take a Deep Breath, Getting Rid of Toxic Waste, Listening to Your Early Warning Signals	Early Warning Signals	Creating a Symbol for True Self, Calming Stressful Feelings, Giving and Receiving Compliments, Journals
5	Learning to Say No	Handling Peer Pressure, Learning to Say No, Persistence, Persistence and Empathy, Supplemental: Negotiating, Keeping the Peace	My Own True Self Stories, Helpful Hints for Saying No to Unfair Requests and Demands	Refuse Unreasonable Requests, Write Your Own True-Self Story, How Do You Handle Criticism?, Compliments?, True-Self Stone Symbols, Journals
6	Mistakes, Criticism, Feelings, and Needs	Admitting Mistakes, Handling Criticism Expressing Feelings and Needs, "I" Language, Fogging, Supplemental: Sandwiching Criticism, Feeling Good Ideas	Helpful Hints: Dealing with Criticism, Expressing Dissatisfaction, Disagreeing, Do You Act or React?	Collecting Jokes, What Would You Say? Offer to Help Someone
7	Social Skills, Integration, Goals	Humor, Conversations, Behavioral Rehearsal, Goals–Aftereffects, Post Self-Assessment, Closing: You're Awesome!, Supplemental: Goal Setting Two	What Life Is All About, Reminder: Step by Step to Responsible Assertion	Feeling Good Two

About the Authors

Laura G. Manis has spent three decades in counseling and personnel work. She has a special interest in developing programs that meet the unique needs of women and girls. She helped to plan and establish the Center for Women's Services and the Women's Studies Program at Western Michigan University.

She has developed a number of programs for women: SEARCH – to help women reassess goals; CONTACT – to help separated and divorced persons readjust; and two programs for school-age women and girls to explore roles, plan ahead, and learn skills for effective living.

Lately, she has devoted her energies to working with caregivers of Alzheimer's patients and other long-term care families. She has trained support-group facilitators, written a trainer's manual for the same group and organized a grassroots coalition to work with the Hawaii State Legislature to develop a financing program to help families pay for long-term care.

Ms. Manis is the author of *Womanpower*, a book that evolved from her work with young women and *Assertion Training Workshop* a result of eight years of teaching assertion skills to a variety of populations and training large numbers of assertion workshop leaders.

Lisa Neela Manis is a hypnotherapist, teacher, a graduate consultant, and an examiner for the American Council of Hypnotherapist Examiners.

She has an extensive background in transformational hypnotherapy, Gestalt, transactional analysis, focusing, and counseling with more than 20 years of human potential training.

She received her bachelors degree from the University of Michigan in Eastern Philosophy and Art and has completed graduate work at the University of Washington in Social Work. She also facilitated group work, and developed a successful skills-development program for teen girls in a group-home setting—The Family Group Homes in Ann Arbor Michigan. She is now in private practice as a hypnotherapist in Santa Fe, New Mexico.

Session 1
What is Assertive Behavior?

Overview

Goals
To give participants an overview of the workshop. To help participants feel comfortable with each other and with the structure and methods used. To learn how to distinguish assertive from nonassertive behavior.

Materials
Name tags, pencils, newsprint, marking pens, Resource Sheets A1-1 through A1-10

Teacher Instructions
Presession Self-Assessment
What Is this Workshop About?
Skill Instruction: Introductions
Workshop Expectations and Procedures – Getting From Here to There
Exercise Instruction: Ice-Breaker – Do You Like String Beans?
Exercise Instruction: Keeping Confidences
Discussion: What Is Assertive Behavior?
Skill Instruction: Your Body Talks Too
Exercise Instruction: Telling the Difference
Skill Instruction: Your Comfort Level
Closing the Session
Supplemental Instruction Activity: The Name Game

Student Resource Sheets
Presession Self-Assessment (A1-1)
Getting From Here to There (A1-2)
Keeping Confidences (A1-3)
What Is Assertive Behavior? (A1-4)
Your Comfort Level (A1-5)
The Link (A1-6)
How Keeping a Journal Helps and True Story 1 (A1-7)
Discrimination Quiz (A1-8)
Homework Activity: Three Things I Did Today (A1-9)
Supplemental Activity: Do I Have Trouble with Any of These? (A1-10)

Homework
Review Getting from Here to There (A1-2)
Review How Keeping a Diary Helps (A1-7)
Homework Activity: Three Things I Did Today (A1-9)
Discrimination Quiz (A1-8)
Supplemental Activity: Do I Have Trouble with Any of These? (A1-10)
Record your reactions in your diary: introduce yourself to three strangers; observe three situations, how did you or others behave (as illustrated in the

example provided in Appendix F); write down three things you accomplished this week.

Presession Self-Assessment

Purpose

- To provide a base line for measuring any behavioral changes.
- To provide an aid to the leader and the participant in identifying the types of behavior that cause difficulties.
- To use as a reference if participants have difficulty thinking of personal situations for role playing.

Materials

Resource Sheet A1-1, pencils

Instruction

- Assessment is an important means of measuring any behavioral changes. The presession assessment can be completed prior to the first session, either at the time of registration or while waiting for the session to start.
- The group leader asks participants to complete the self-assessment sheet and to bring it to each session.
- Instruct them to decide the areas that they would like to practice changing. These will be useful for them to use later if they have trouble thinking of where they need improvement.
- At the end of the seven sessions they will be asked to complete a similar post-session sheet and then compare the two in order to see how they have improved and also what might need further practice.

Notes

◆ What Is This Workshop About?

⏲ 10 minutes

Purpose

- To introduce participants to the purpose of the workshop.
- To explain the method of training.
- To show how being assertive increases self-esteem.

Materials

- Newsprint, marking pens

Discussion

- The group leader welcomes participants and explains that she will wait to have introductions in a little bit because it is part of the training.
- The leader then explains that learning how to say what you mean and to stand up for yourself, is called assertive behavior and helps you feel better about yourself—self-esteem.
- Being responsible is also part of assertive behavior and that means that while we wish our rights to be respected when we are assertive, we also respect the rights of other.
- The leader draws the illustration below on newsprint or on the blackboard to show how a vicious circle is created when inadequate behavior affects self-esteem. Then change "inadequate" to "adequate," "negative" to "positive," and "lower" to "higher" self-esteem to graphically illustrate the impact of changing behavior.

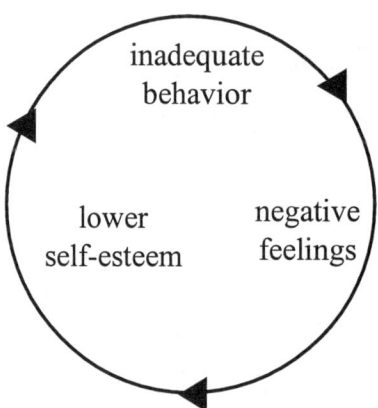

- The leader then makes the following points:
  » Being assertive does not necessarily mean getting your way. Quite often it means working out an acceptable compromise.

4

- How can you tell if you have been assertive? If you have doubts, ask yourself whether what you said or how you acted made you feel good even slightly. If it did, it was assertive.
- The goal we are aiming for is to become assertive. We may have difficulty with certain persons or in certain situations. However as long as we proceed in small steps and feel ourselves increasing in self-esteem, we will feel better about ourselves and have greater control over our lives.
- The first few sessions will include practice using situations the leader will choose. The last few will be practice of situations with which the participants have difficulty.
- The workshop will have four training steps (Resource Sheet A1-2).
  - » Learning to tell assertive behavior from aggressive and nonassertive behaviors.
  - » Identifying personal rights and accepting them as well as respecting the rights of others.
  - » Reducing blocks to acting assertively.
  - » Developing skills through role playing and practice.

Skill Instruction: Introductions

⏱ 15 minutes

Purpose
- To introduce the participants to each other.
- To practice being assertive in a simple, familiar situation.

Discussion
- In most groups, when people first get together, there is a time when each person, in turn, tells who they are and a few things about themselves. We will do that also. This is a good way to practice being assertive.
- When it is your turn, say your name. Say it so everyone hears you, don't mumble. Then say some things that will help tell who you are. Because we are still pretty much strangers, you shouldn't expect to tell very personal things about yourself or your innermost secrets; that would not be appropriate. However, it is appropriate to tell your name, grade, your school, age, and why you are in this group. (Or say one thing you like to do or is important to you.)
- It is assertive to look at people when you talk, not at the floor, or the ceiling, or out the window. Let your gaze fall on different people as you introduce yourself.
- Let's take a few minutes to think of what to say before you speak. Now imagine yourself saying it assertively to the group (hidden rehearsal).

Procedure
- Have participants seated in a circle facing each other.
- Tell the participants that whenever you go around the circle in some activities, you will always start on your left (or right). This lets that person know what to expect and time to prepare to speak.
- Start the exercise by introducing yourself. You might tell how you felt at their age and a bit about the problems you had being assertive.
- After each person speaks, give positive feedback on at least one assertive component in that person's delivery (e.g., eye contact, body language, voice control, pitch, conciseness).
- Invite the other participants to give positive comments also.

Notes

✑ Workshop Expectations and Procedures
Getting From Here to There

🕒 5 minutes

Purpose
- To have participants learn what to expect from the workshop and how it is to be accomplished.
- To tell participants what is expected of them and of the leaders.

Materials
- Resource Sheet A1-2

Discussion

The leader reviews the expectations and the procedures with the group and answers any questions.

Expectations and Outcomes for Participants

Based on attendance and participation in all seven sessions of the workshop, it is expected you will:

- decide which are the situations where you would like to be to be able to express yourself assertively (from self-assessment page)
- be able to distinguish assertive behavior from aggressive and nonassertive behavior
- examine and clarify your beliefs about your rights and those of the people with whom you are communicating
- understand how those rights are related to assertive behavior
- learn how certain feelings make it difficult to be assertive but easy to be aggressive or nonassertive
- have several opportunities to practice standing up for your opinions and needs without violating the rights of others
- feel stronger, respected, and more in control of your life
- be free to refuse to participate in any activity, no reasons need to be given as long as you do so in a manner that does not interfere with the choices and participation of other members
- keep a daily diary of the results of your practice behavior (homework) outside of the workshop and record in your diary, feelings, thoughts, ideas, and opinions
- keep confidential any information discussed in the group

Expectations for Workshop Leader(s)

It is expected that the leader(s) will:

- use education and training skills to teach assertive behavior
- provide practice of assertive skills during sessions
- teach skills to reduce blocks to assertive behavior
- be prepared, model assertive behavior and be present every week
- respect the right of any participant to refuse to participate in any activity as long as it doesn't interfere with the participation of the other members
- keep confidential any information discussed in the group

Methods and Procedures

We will meet for about two hours a week for seven weeks during which our sessions will include:

- discussions, demonstrations, questionnaires, paper-and-pencil exercises, short homework assignments, and behavior rehearsals or role-playing.
- focus on behaviors such as dealing with criticism and "put-downs," persistence, asking for help or favors, saying "no" to unreasonable requests, resisting what makes us uncomfortable or guilty, making reasonable compromises, and expressing opinions

Exercise Instruction
Ice-Breaker – Do You Like String Beans?

⏲ 5 minutes

Purpose
- To help participants relax, have fun, loosen up, let off steam.
- To start getting to know each other by doing a nonthreatening exercise.
- To make it easier for participants to respond to each other and the leaders by increasing feelings of safety and group cohesiveness.

Procedure
- Ask the participants to imagine a line representing a progression from one to 10. Mark two locations in the room.
- State that one point represents one, meaning "not at all," while the other point represents 10 meaning "a great deal."
- Ask the participants to place themselves on the line according to how well they like the following items. Ask each of the questions below:
    » "How well do you like string beans"
    » "How well do you like asparagus?"
    » "How well do you like the color purple?"
    » "How well do you like the color yellow?"
    » "How well do you like Chinese food?"
    » "How well do you like Italian food?"
    » "How well do you like cats?"
    » "How well do you like dogs?"
    » "How well do you like big parties?"
    » "How well do you like small get-togethers?"
    » "How well do you like _____?"
    (Whatever the leader chooses; homework, gym class, pizza, rap music, chocolate, reading, writing.)
    » "How assertive do you rate yourself?"

Notes

❧ Exercise Instruction: Keeping Confidences

🕐 20 minutes

Purpose

- To demonstrate the importance of confidentiality in building trust.
- To show how revealing secrets harms friendships and lowers the self-esteem of both the revealer and the gossiper.

Materials

- The vignette on Resource Sheet A1-3.

Discussion

- The leaders discuss the importance of not telling parents or friends about anything that happens in the workshop in order to create a safe, comfortable place where members can say whatever they like or feel.
- It is okay to tell about what the exercises are or what you learned but do not reveal specific situations or mention names.
- This is true in real life also. If you want your friends to trust you, you don't break confidences.
- There is an exception to this rule. If the secret involves physical harm to themselves or others, you must tell someone in authority.
- Discuss briefly who are the persons you can tell (your parents, teachers, counselors).
- Right now we will do a role play to show the effects of breaking confidences.

Procedure

- Ask for three volunteers, one to be the person with the secret, Karla, one to act the friend, Brittany, one to be the third person, Megan. Use Resource Sheet A1-3.

> *Megan is offstage. Brittany is in the group.*

Karla: I dropped my books in the hall yesterday and this real cool guy picked them up for me. He was so cute and so nice! His name is Josh and he sits two rows ahead of me in home room. I have been seeing Brian but now I think I like Josh better. I'm thinking I will drop Brian. But I don't know how to tell him.

> *Karla leaves.*
> *Next day, Brittany a member of the group, meets Megan:*

Megan: Hey, how's the group going?

Brittany: Just great. Yesterday my friend, Karla wanted to know how to dump Brian because she just met this great guy Josh.

Megan: Really. Hmmm, that's interesting.

> *Brittany leaves. Karla arrives.*

Megan: Hey, Karla I just heard you were going to dump Brian. Mind if I ask him to the movies?

> *Megan leaves. Brittany arrives. Karla greets Brittany.*

Karla: You weren't supposed to tell anyone about what's said in the group. How come you did that? I thought you were my friend.

- Leader asks: How is Karla going to feel about saying anything in the group again. Will she come back?
- Karla, how did you feel when you heard that your secret had spread. Did it affect your self-esteem? How did you feel about your friend?
- Brittany, how did you feel after you told Karla's secret to someone else. What about after Karla told you, "I thought you were my friend?"
- Does anyone in the group have any reactions?

◆◦ Discussion: What Is Assertive Behavior?

⏱ 20 Minutes

Purpose
- To learn what assertiveness behavior is.
- To learn how to tell the difference between assertive behavior and nonassertive behavior.
- To understand some reasons that keep people from being assertive.

Materials
- Resource Sheet A1-4

Discussion
- The group leaders asks "What does being assertive mean to you?" and without comment lists all replies on newsprint.
- After all replies are listed, say something positive such as "that's a very good list to start with." Now let's look at the approved definition and turn to Resource Sheet A1-4.

Definition

Read out loud: assertive behavior means standing up for yourself without hurting others. You can say what you think, feel, and believe in a direct, confident, honest, and suitable way without hurting others.

Examples:

- I don't want to see violent movies any more. How about if we find one we can both like or we do something else.
- Your friend telephones you and wants to change the plans you two have decided on for an evening together. You say, Wow, this is really a surprise. I'd like to call you back as soon as I have time to think about this.
- Leader asks group to analyze the examples:
    » How were they assertive?
    » Were they direct?
    » Did they say what they felt?
    » Did they hurt the other person?
- The group leader asks the group to define aggressive behavior and again lists the replies on a new sheet of newsprint.

Definition

Read out loud: *aggressive behavior* goes to extreme. People who are aggressive must get their way without regard for the feelings or rights of other people. They stand up for themselves all right but they want to win or dominate and end up making the other person feel insulted, humiliated, angry, and confused.

Examples:

- You just love violence don't you. There must be something wrong with people like you who go to movies like that!
- You are the most inconsiderate, thoughtless person I've ever seen! You just never think of me, just selfish all the time.
- Leader asks group:
    » What is the message they are getting across?
    » Isn't it "I'm better than you, you are stupid, selfish etc. even though they said what they thought.
- Group leader now asks for the group's definition of nonassertive behavior and lists them on paper.

Definition

Read out loud: *nonassertive or passive* people let others make decisions for them. They don't say what they want, sometimes don't know what they want or speak in such an apologetic, cautious, nonconfident manner that they are ignored.

Examples:

- When you let someone talk you into something you don't want to do. Your friend wants to watch a football game on TV. There is something else you would rather watch. You say, "Well, ah, sure, oh, okay.
- When you let yourself be ignored when you try to give your opinion. Your friends are discussing where to go after school. Every time you suggest something, no one seems to hear you. Finally, you just give up.
- What message are you sending to people?
    » I don't count.
    » I'm not worth listening to.
    » You can take advantage of me.

There is another kind of nonassertive behavior that combines passive or nonassertive behavior with aggressive behavior. Its called passive-aggressive behavior.

Definition

Read out loud: *passive-aggressive* behavior means not standing up for yourself at first and then sabotaging the situation later so that the other person feels guilty, punished, or angry.

Examples:

- Your friend wants to watch a football game on TV. There is something else you would rather watch. You say, "Well, ah, sure, go ahead and watch the game. (Then you talk loudly and constantly through the whole game.)
- A cousin calls and asks if she can stay with you this weekend. You have never liked her but your mother says you must be nice to her. You say, "Sure, come." However during her visit you are cross and complain constantly.
- Your mother asks you to deliver something important to a friend. You wanted to do something else, but you agree, then "forget" to deliver the thing, lose it, or break it on the way.
  - » What's the message? "I did what you asked, didn't I. So I can't be punished if it didn't work out."

Notes

Skill Instruction: Your Body Talks Too

⏲ 15 minutes

Purpose
- To stimulate awareness of nonverbal communication as part of the message.
- To learn the importance of having the verbal and nonverbal messages be the same.

Materials
- Newsprint and markers

Discussion
- The leader tells the participants that besides the words we use we also communicate with our bodies and our facial expressions.
- The leader demonstrates saying "I want to see this movie," as follows.

Procedure
- *Aggressive* behavior: Stand very close to a participant, glare at her, speak loudly, clench your fists, or shake a finger at her.
  » Ask participants what kind of behavior this was (aggressive, nonassertive, passive-aggressive, or assertive) and how could they tell? How did her eyes look? Brows? Mouth? Position? Hands? Anything else?
  » List responses to the question "How could they tell?" on newsprint.

Follow procedure as above for the nonassertive, assertive, and passive-aggressive examples, using the same statement.

- *Nonassertive* behavior: Stand a distance away, body turned slightly away, soft hesitant voice, wring hands, look down, mumble.
- *Assertive:* Stand at comfortable distance, about three feet away, look directly at the person, hands relaxed, speak clearly and firmly.
- *Passive-aggressive:* Say the statement nonassertively, then act hurt and say "you never listen to me." Or some other statement that makes the other person feel guilty or hurt or angry.

Notes

☙ Exercise Instruction: Telling the Difference

🕒 10 minutes

Purpose
- To identify the different types of behavior.
- To help correct any misunderstandings.

Discussion
- Leaders review the definitions of behavior on Resource Sheet A1-4.
- Discuss the exercise as follows: "We are going to listen to a series of statements concerning a situation. The statement may be assertive, aggressive, nonassertive, or passive-aggressive. Afterwards, I will ask you what your answer is. I will be particularly interested if any of you see the statement differently from the rest. You may be right, you know. This will give me a chance to clear up whatever confusion there is about these different behaviors."

Procedure
- Read aloud the situations below.
- After each statement ask if it is assertive, nonassertive, aggressive, or passive-aggressive.
- If a participant misidentifies a situation, start the discussion by saying "What was it about the response that caused you to see it as _____?"
- Other questions to ask are: "How do the others see it?" "Are you saying to yourself that someone wouldn't like you if you said that?" "Are you assuming that everybody reacts like you do?"
- Repeat the above steps for each of the following situations.

Situation 1
- At a party where you don't know anyone except the hostess, you want to circulate and get to know others. You walk up to three people who are talking.
    » You stand close to them and smile but say nothing, waiting for them to notice you (nonassertive).
    » You wait for a pause in the conversation, introduce yourself, and comment on the subject (assertive).
    » You listen to the subject they are talking about, then break in and say loudly, "You are absolutely wrong about that" (aggressive).

Situation 2
- You've borrowed a blouse from your sister without telling her and somehow spilled something down the front that won't come out.

- » You say to your sister when she sees the blouse, "Well, I didn't do it on purpose did I, it was an accident. Besides the blouse was dirty anyway, you should have put it in the laundry (aggressive).
- » You tell your sister about it and apologize, telling her you feel awful and want to figure out something to make up for it (assertive).
- » You put the blouse in the garbage, don't say anything and pretend you don't know anything when she can't find it (passive-aggressive).
- » You hang it back up without saying anything (nonassertive).

Situation 3

- Your friends want you to go to a party where you know they will be smoking pot and drinking. You feel uncomfortable about going.
    - » You go anyway because you want your friends to like you but you feel miserable the whole time (nonassertive).
    - » You tell your friends they shouldn't be doing those things and are stupid if they go to the party (aggressive).
    - » You tell your friends you feel uncomfortable going because of the pot and the drinking, and would rather do other things with them and no, you've decided not to go (assertive).
    - » You go to the party, act critical, and complain about what a lousy party it is, why did they make you go (passive-aggressive).

⚡ Skill Instruction: Your Comfort Level

⏲ 5 Minutes

Purpose

- To help participants become aware of their anxieties.
- To be able to judge the intensity of the feelings.
- To demonstrate how the levels can change and be used in measuring successful assertion.

Materials

- Chalkboard or newsprint, markers, Resource Sheet A1-5

Procedure

- Read the following to the participants:
  » Imagine a scene where you are completely relaxed and calm. For some people this may be while lying on a sunny beach or on a mountain top. For others, this may be while reading a good book or riding a bicycle.
  » Give your feelings in the most relaxed situation a score of "0."
- Next, imagine a situation where you are completely panic stricken. It may be speaking before a large group or taking an exam. Your hands are clammy, you feel shaky, your heart is pounding, and your brain is paralyzed.
  » Give the feeling you experience in this situation a score of "100."
- You have now identified the two end-points of your comfort level—zero and 100. Imagine the entire scale like a ruler, going by 10's from zero (completely relaxed) to 100 (extremely anxious).
- Draw on the chalkboard or newsprint the scale below to illustrate.

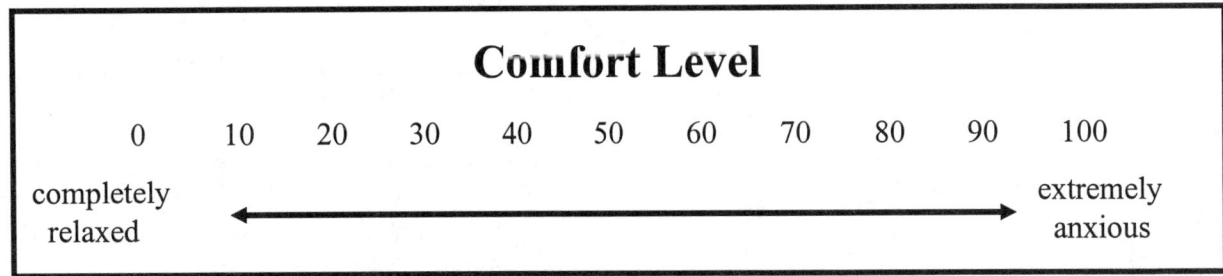

- Look at the participants and say mildly, "What is your comfort level?"
- After the participants have identified their comfort level, yell loudly and directly at a participant: "What is it now! This very minute!." (The participant usually responds with a much higher level, showing that people can easily discriminate between high and low comfort levels.)

Discussion

- Discuss the use of the scale as follows:
    » The comfort level scale will be used throughout the assertion-training program. After responding to each situation in which you have practiced assertive behavior, note your level in your diary. A goal of repeated assertive practice is to lower your anxiety as much as possible since anxiety can keep you from saying what you want and can interfere with the way you deliver your message. However, you will always have some anxiety with certain people or in certain situations. For example, telling your teacher that you think she made a mistake is an anxiety-producing experience. Therefore, your goal is not to reduce your comfort level to zero or 10 in all situations, but to reduce your comfort level to where you feel relaxed enough to express yourself. High levels of anxiety are unpleasant for most people.

◆ Closing the Session

⏲ 10 minutes

Purpose
- To bring closure to the session
- To integrate the exercises with the cognitive material
- To allow evaluation by the leader

Materials
- Newsprint or chalkboard with the phrases listed in The Link (Resource Sheet A1-6) to be used at the end of each session

Discussion
- You will have some simple homework to do before we meet for the next session.

Homework
📖 Readings
- True Story 1 – Lisa's Story (A1-7)
- Review Getting from Here to There (A1-2)
- What is Assertive Behavior (A1-4)
- How Keeping a Diary Helps (A1-7)
    » use a notebook to record feelings, reactions, ideas as we go through the workshop
    » if you wish you may want to share what you wrote during homework reviews

◎ Activities
- Complete Discrimination Quiz (Resource Sheet A1-8)
- Introduce yourself to three strangers.
- Record your behavior in your journal.
- Notice how you and others behave toward each other and record in your journal as illustrated in the example (Appendix F). At this point, you are learning to identify the different kinds of behavior—not practice them. Observe three situations.
- Write down three things you have accomplished this week (A1-9). Did you clean your room, make your bed, do school homework? Remember the small accomplishments.

Procedure for The Link (A1-6) Exercise
- The leader tells the participants to think about today's session and complete the phrase that best summarizes their feelings.
- We will go around the group so that each person has a turn.

- Have each participant complete a phrase.
- These phrases are all assertive statements and can be used to express opinions and needs elsewhere.

The Link

✻ Today I learned that . . .

✻ I wish that . . .

✻ Right now I feel . . .

✻ I was pleased . . .

✻ This session helped me to . . .

✻ I will think more about . . .

✻ What I like about myself is . . .

✻ Next time I'd like to . . .

Notes

⇜ Supplemental Instruction: The Name Game

🕒 5 minutes

Purpose
- To provide a creative activity as the group gathers.
- To help participants learn each others names.
- To start group cohesiveness.

Materials
- Large self-adhesive name tags, or colored paper and pins if needed, colored markers.

Procedure
- As each girl arrives ask them to create their own name tag. The gummed labels should be large enough to be seen easily.
- Have them pick colored markers, create a design with their first name. The leaders already are wearing theirs as a model.
- Ask everyone to stand in a circle so that each person's name tag can be seen.
- Since sometimes the girls have unusual names, go around the circle and have them say their own name out loud so that everyone can hear how it is pronounced.
- If two girls have the same name, ask them what they would like to be called.
- To start the game one of the leaders claps her hands and says a name and points at the girl whose name she calls.
- Then the first girl claps and points at another girl and says her name.
- Continue until you build up speed and it sounds like you are all clapping together.
- Finish by saying that later in this session, we will go around the circle and find out a little more about each other. This time we just wanted to learn each others names and how to pronounce them.

Notes

Supplemental Instruction:
Do I Have Trouble with Any of These?

🕓 5 minutes

Purpose

- A simpler pre/post session assessment sheet to use with younger girls or if time is limited.
- To identify problem areas for further examination.
- To provide a baseline for measuring changes.

Materials

- Resource Sheet A1-10, pencils

Procedure

- Assessment is an important means of measuring any behavioral changes. The presession assessment can be completed prior to the first session, either at the time of registration or while waiting for the session to start.
- The group leader asks participants to complete the page and to bring it to each session.
- Instruct them to decide the areas that they would like to practice changing. These will be useful for them to use later if they have trouble thinking of where they need improvement.
- At the end of the seven sessions they will be asked to complete a similar post-session sheet and them compare the two in order to see how they have improved and also what might need further practice.

Notes

Session 2
Identifying Feelings

Overview

Goal
To learn to recognize feelings, identify them, and use them as an important base for becoming assertive, knowing themselves, developing group cohesiveness, and improving personal relationships.

Materials
Newsprint or chalk board, sheets of adhesive labels about 2" x 4" with enough labels on each sheet for each member in the group, colored marking pens, one blank sheet of construction paper for each girl, pins, Resource Sheets A2-1 through A2-8, diary.

Teacher Instructions
Homework Review
Skill Instruction: Desensitization to Eye Contact
Skill Instruction: Listening and Hearing
Skill Instruction: Name that Feeling
Skill Instruction: What Do I Like to Do?
Skill Exercise: What Do I Like About Myself?
Skill Instruction: Giving and Receiving Compliments
Exercise Instruction: Compliment Scramble
Closing the Session

Student Resource Sheets
True Story 2: I Like Me (A2-1)
Listening and Hearing (A2-2)
Name That Feeling (A2-3)
What Do I Like To Do? (A2-4)
What Do I Like About Myself? (A2-5)
Get to Your Point (A2-6)
Supplemental Exercise: Deeper Listening (A2-7)
Supplemental Exercise: All About Me (A2-8)

Homework
Read: True Story 2 – I Like Me (A2-1)
Read: Listening and Hearing (A2-2)
Complete Get to Your Point (A2-6)
Supplemental Activity: Deeper Listening (A2-7)
Supplemental Activity: All About Me (A2-8)

❧ Homework Review

⏲ 15 minutes

Purpose
- To evaluate understanding of concepts introduced in previous session.
- To see if further practice is needed.
- To provide positive feedback at first attempts of assertive behavior.

Materials
- Resource sheets A1–1 through A1-10, journal sheets (Appendix F), diary

Procedure
- All sessions should start with a homework review. The leaders may wish to use the format suggested below.
- Check the journals while the group is gathering. Were incidents recorded correctly? If time is short, the leader may wish to collect the journals to review and to comment in writing. Provide extra journal sheets if necessary.
- Ask for the participants' reactions to the homework assignment. Ask questions such as:
  » How did you feel when you introduced yourself to three strangers?
  » What were their reactions to you?
  » Did you have any problems recognizing the different kinds of behavior?
- Provide the correct answers to the Discrimination Quiz (A1-8). Discuss any questionable items.
  1. N; **2.** AG; **3.** A; **4.** PAG; **5.** AG; **6.** A; **7.** AG; **8.** A; **9.** A; **10.** N
- Ask for reports of successful assertion. Remind the participants that at this point being able to speak up when they want to is the goal and that successful assertion does not necessarily mean that they must have "won" or made things happen their way.
- If participants are not satisfied with their assertive experiences, review the experiences before the group. Ask such questions as:
  » What did you want to accomplish?
  » What are the actual words you used?
  » What would you have liked to say?
  » Could it have been said better?
  » What was your body language?
  » Was the situation too complicated?
  » Did the other person react to how you used to behave in the past rather than your new behavior?
  » Are you feeling guilty needlessly?
  » Why do you think the experience was not assertive?

- » Did you give in at the first sign of resistance?
- Remind the participants that even if their attempts at being assertive were not successful, they should be proud of their efforts to speak up and making their thoughts and wishes known (see Resource Sheet A2-1)
- Learning to be assertive is a skill like typing. It takes practice to get better.

❧ Skill Instruction: Desensitization to Eye Contact

🕒 5 minutes

Purpose

- To help participants learn how to maintain eye contact in assertive and social situations.
- To overcome cultural barriers to maintaining eye contact.

Discussion

- Leaders discuss eye contact as follows:
    - » I've noticed that some of you have trouble making eye contact. Since eye contact is an important part of becoming assertive and part of your body-language message, it is important that you develop this ability.
    - » If you have this trouble, it could be because you were taught that where your family came from, it was not polite to look people in the eye. However, here it may be mistaken for being nonassertive.
    - » Or, maybe when you were about two years old and could not understand language very well, it may have seemed like a very large person in a loud voice pointed two very large light beams that saw way down into your soul and boomed, "Who did that?" You looked away and hoped you were invisible. This exercise helps desensitize you to that early fear.

Procedure

- Have the participants pick a partner and face her about four feet away. This can be done sitting or standing.
- Tell one of the pairs to look at their partner's right ankle, left knee, right hip, breast bone, left shoulder, right shoulder, chin, left ear, right ear, forehead, right temple, and finally into her eyes.
- Have the partner take a turn doing the same.
- Next, have the participants take turns looking into their partners eyes and very slowly look away. Ask the partner to sit with her hand at shoulder level and raise a finger as soon as she can tell when their eyes are out of contact.
- Say to the group:
    - » For those of you who have a difficult time starting and maintaining eye contact, you will notice that at a distance of four feet, a person can't tell whether you are looking her in the eye or at her ear. Talk to their ears or forehead if it helps you feel more comfortable.

Notes

Skill Instruction: Listening and Hearing

🕐 30 minutes

Purpose
- To teach the skill of listening.
- To improve personal relationships.

Materials
- Listening and Hearing, Resource A2-2

Discussion
- The leaders introduce the exercise by telling the group, "We will be talking to each other a lot during this workshop so it is important that we learn how to listen. Being a good listener also is part of learning to be assertive. It will help you in social situations and in person relationships. One problem is that we are often so busy preparing a reply that we do not hear what is really being said."
- We can improve our listening by practicing certain skills described in this exercise.

Procedure
- Leader starts exercise by asking "Can you remember a time when you were with a group or with a person and could not seem to make yourself heard? What happened? How did you feel?"
- After a brief discussion say, "We are going to break up the listening process into easy steps."

Step one is called "attending" or paying attention.

- Now form into groups of three—a *listener*, a *speaker*, and an *observer*.
- Before the triads start, the leaders should demonstrate the exercise with the group members being the observers and giving feedback.
- The *speaker* selects a topic from the list below to discuss for one minute.
    » How do you feel about getting out of bed in the morning?
    » Do you have any trouble deciding what to wear every day?
    » Does your mom complain about how you dress?
    » Who listens to you best, your mom or dad?
    » Pick an easy topic of your own to talk about?
- The *listener* at this point is to concentrate on only listening and does not reply.
    » She faces the speaker.
    » She may lean forward slightly.
    » She meets the listener's eyes.
    » Her only response is to nod her head or say "uh huh" at intervals.

- The *observer* keeps the time and after the one minute is up gives feedback or tells the listener how she did. Watch for the four points above. Start with what was well done and then if necessary add one thing that can be improved.
- Each person takes a turn being *speaker, listener,* and *observer.*
- After each has had a turn, leaders ask the groups how it felt being listened to this way.
    - » Was it different?
    - » Was it hard to keep quiet when you were the listener?
    - » Did you think of anything while you were listening?

Step two adds a reply.

- This time, in the same groups of three, the *listener* can reply but only by repeating what the speaker has said, trying to be exact.
- The leaders should demonstrate again.
- The *speaker* can talk about the same topic, pick another from the list or choose her own. She should pause occasionally to give the listener time to respond.
- The *observer* again keeps time and then gives feedback. Did the listener look attentive, Was she able to repeat what the listener said?
- After the exercise the leaders ask the groups if there were any problems?
    - » Was there any difficulty in parroting the speaker?
    - » What interfered?

Step three is called active listening.

- The *speaker* again picks a topic and talks for one minute pausing for comments.
- This time, instead of parroting the exact words of the speaker, the *listener* summarizes what the speaker said in her own words. It is helpful to preface your summary with words like "I think you said . . . " or "I understood you to say . . . "
- Don't hesitate to say you don't understand something if that is so. This gives the speaker a chance to correct any misunderstandings and at the same time clarify her own thoughts. (Very helpful to the process.)
- The *observer* keeps time and gives feedback on how well the listener followed the guidelines. Notice anything else about either the speaker or the listener that either obstructs or helps the interaction.
- After the observer gives her report, the three participants may want to discuss the exchange briefly.
- Members change roles until each has experienced each role.
- Discuss, in the group as a whole:
    - » What seemed to be the behavior that most interfered with discussing the topic?
    - » Did having to summarize before responding affect the listener in any way?
    - » Did it affect the speaker?

- To understand what actually happens during a conversation, read the "Listening But Not Really Hearing" description on Resource Sheet A2-2.

Notes

❧ Skill Instruction: Name That Feeling

🕐 20 minutes

Purpose
- To increase knowledge of feeling words.
- To encourage expressing feelings in a nonthreatening way.

Materials
- Newsprint or chalkboard, markers, Resource Sheet A2-3

Discussion
- Lead into the next exercise by saying that when they recorded their comfort level, they were thinking about how they felt. That before you can change a feeling, you must first identify it—what it is called—so that you can talk about it.
- Talking about it, or just saying what it is can be a great relief. You get it out in the open, outside of your head so that you can think more clearly.
- Saying how you feel is also an important part of your assertive message.
- Explain that there may be comfortable and enjoyable or uncomfortable feelings but they are not "good" or "bad." Everyone has feelings, they are part of being human.
- Sometimes we feel miserable because we carry around a feeling, try to hide it, have trouble putting a name on it, and take it out on everyone around us.
- Talking about our feelings can relieve them, and clear our heads so that we can decide what to do. It also helps people understand why we are acting a certain way and deepens relationships.
- Some people have tried to bury their feelings for so long, they have forgotten what they are. These people can look and act like robots, or they always act angry but don't know why.
- We have many feelings during a day. Let's talk about some of them.

Procedure
- The leader writes the word "feeling" on newsprint. The group leader points to different participants who stand up and call out a feeling. The leader lists them on the newsprint.
- Be careful to distinguish between thoughts and feelings.
- Explain that before you can change a feeling, you must first identify it.
- After they have suggested at least 10 feelings, ask each person to pick a feeling and describe a situation where they experienced the feeling. Example: I was *embarrassed* when I came late to class and everyone looked at me.
- Ask the person whether the feeling changed after they said the word.
- Did anything happen to you today that you are still feeling concerned about. Pick a feeling that describes it.

- Below are some feeling words to add to the list, if they run out of them.

scared	excited	happy	embarrassed	proud	sad
confused	worried	relieved	glad	put down	content
angry	lonely	in control	bored	grateful	frustrated
miserable	capable	powerful	peaceful	affectionate	loving
delighted	cool	uptight	bitter	grouchy	bold
nervous	irritated	frightened	ashamed	guilty	regretful

- On Resource Sheet A2-3 is Janelle's short story. After you have read it, list the feelings the writer has expressed.
- Next, complete the feelings, situation, and what do I say section.
- The leaders should demonstrate first by telling each other a feeling, the situation and describing it as in this example: "I felt embarrassed when I came late to class and everyone looked at me."
- Turn to the person on your right and take turns telling each other the feeling, situation, and what you could say. Be sure to make eye contact when you talk.
- Group discussion:
    » Was it hard to tell your partner how you felt?
    » Did your feeling change in any way after you talked about it?

Notes

Skill Instruction: What Do I Like to Do?

⏲ 10 minutes

Purpose
- To start to identify positive traits.
- To develop a strategy for raising self-esteem.

Materials
- Resource Sheet A2-4, colored pens or crayons.

Procedure

This strategy uses three steps as described below. Step 1 is becoming aware of the things the participants *like to do,* step two is recognizing what they *like about themselves*. Step 3 is being bombarded with *compliments* from group members. Below are the instructions for Step 1.

- Ask the participants to think of at least three things they like (a feeling word) to do.
- It could be something they do in their spare time. For example, do they like to listen to music, dance, read, draw, be outdoors, sports, play games, hang out with friends?
- Ask them to draw a picture or a symbol of some of the things they like to do in the space on their sheet (A2-4). Tell them, "Draw it any way you like. Don't draw anything fancy, we only have about five minutes to do this."
- Tell them that after they have finished, everyone in the group will show their picture to the group and explain it. That they don't have to worry about what it looks like, we're not trying to make works of art.
- The leader(s) show a prepared picture they have drawn about their likes to show that it isn't a work of art. It can be stick figures or symbols like a flower, a music note, a book or the sun.
- After everyone finishes their picture, the leaders start discussion by saying, "I will start. It's easier for me because I've had more time to think about this. I'm going to do this assertively, by looking at everyone when I talk and speaking clearly."
- After the leader speaks, she will go around the group (circles are best) telling them she will start on her left (or right) if that's how she has done it previously.

Discussion

- Discuss the following questions with the participants after all have spoken.
    » Is it hard to talk about yourselves?
    » How did we learn this?
- The leader concludes the exercise with a positive statement to the group such as, "It was great hearing what you like. It made me feel that I know you better and you all have so many different and interesting things that you do!"

Skill Exercise: What Do I Like About Myself?

🕐 10 minutes

Purpose
- To help identify positive traits.
- To continue developing a strategy for raising self-esteem.

Materials
Resource Sheet A2-5, markers or crayons.

Procedure
- Now, Step 2, ask participants to think of at least two things they *like* about themselves.
- Say:
  » "They should be things about which you are willing to receive compliments. They could be something about your appearance, your personality, what you do well. For example, are you a good listener, are you good at a sport, can you walk or run for miles, have you ever won a prize, are you a good cook, are you a good baby sitter, or dancer?"
  » "Draw a picture of one of the things you like about yourself in the space on the sheet. Don't make anything fancy, we only have five minutes to do this."
  » "After you have finished everyone will show their pictures to the group and explain it. Don't worry about what they look like, just so you know what they stand for."
- The leader(s) also draws a new picture or has one ready to show to give an idea of how simple the drawings can be—stick figures or symbols that represent what they like—stars, circles, butterflies, books, etc.
- After everyone finishes their picture, the leader starts the discussion by saying, "I will start."
- After the leader speaks, she will go around the group telling them she will start on her left (or right) if that's how she has done it previously.

Discussion
- Discuss the following questions with the participants after all have spoken.
  » Why is it so hard to say anything nice about ourselves?
  » How did we learn this?
  » Why is it necessary to sometimes be able to make positive statements about yourself (e.g., job interviews, starting conversations, volunteering, social relationships)?
- Examples:
  » "I am good at that, I'll do it."
  » "I think being on time is important."
  » "I like to dance too, let's go together."

» Why should anyone like you or believe in you if you do not even like or believe in yourself?

Skill Exercise: Giving and Receiving Compliments

⏲ 15 minutes

Purpose

- To show that positive interactions also involve assertive behavior.
- To help participants learn how to give and receive compliments assertively.
- To facilitate positive, supportive group interaction.
- To increase self-worth.

Discussion

- Discuss giving and receiving compliments as follows:
    » Many nonassertive and aggressive people have difficulty both giving and receiving compliments. Being assertive includes being able to express positive feelings and opinions.
    » Specific enthusiastic and sincere feedback is helpful and builds confidence and is important in any relationship—parent-child, friend-friend, employer-employee—because they improve the relationship and enrich communication and unity.
- There are several ways *not* to respond to compliments. If you use one of these responses you make it unlikely that you will get another compliment from this person.
    » Act out denying shyly, "Oh gosh, who me?" (Implies you must be wrong.)
    » Returning the focus: "Oh, I like your skirt too."
    » Rejecting: "You like this rag? I've had it for ages!"
    » Egotistical: "Yeah, I'm really terrific!"
    » Put down: "Well, you finally said something good."
- There are also negative ways of *giving* a compliment:
    » Sarcastic: "Those pants really do fit well, don't they."
    » Back-handed: "You finally cut your hair, it looks great now."
- We are frequently told not to brag because it is conceited. There is a difference between healthy pride ("Thank you, I'm glad you liked my report. I spent a lot of time preparing it.") and being conceited ("What did you expect? I always do well.") which tries to impress and "one-up" others.

Procedure

- Ask the participants to stand in a circle. Ask alternate participants to give a genuine compliment to the person on the right.
- The compliment can be something that has been mentioned in previous exercises, or something else: appearance, sensitivity, manner, or sincerity.
- Have the receiver respond to the compliment. Suggest the following: "Thank you, that makes me feel good," or "I'm glad you like it, I like it too," or "Thank you for noticing."

- Take a minute to think about what you will say and visualize yourself saying it.
- After the first compliments, have the receiver give a compliment to the person on her right.
- After the compliments are completed, ask that each person go around the circle again and briefly ask each complimenter to tell the receiver something she specifically liked about how the receiver responded to the compliment.
- Make sure the feedback is given directly to the participant.
- People vary in their levels of comfort when giving or receiving compliments. The group might be encouraged to discuss their reactions during the exercise.
- Encourage them to practice this skill in future sessions. They will also be asked to practice as homework with people outside of the group and record how it went in their journals.

Exercise Instruction: Compliment Scramble

⏰ 15 minutes

Purpose
- To raise self-esteem.
- To increase communication skills.
- To create group support and cohesiveness.

Materials
- Sheets of adhesive labels about 2" x 4" with enough labels on each sheet for each member in the group. Colored marking pens. Blank sheet of construction paper for each girl, pins.

Procedure
- Each girl will pin the construction paper to the back of the person sitting on their right.
- The leaders ask every person to write one compliment for each person in the group on a label. It can be something they like about how they look, talk, act, or have said.
- After they have all finished, they will all get up at the same time and paste their labels on the appropriate person's sheet of construction paper.
- When all labels are distributed, they return to their seats.
- Each person then reads out loud the labels of the person on their right until every person's labels are read.

Discussion
- Ask:
  » How did it feel to write the compliments?
  » How did it feel to give the compliments to the other person?
  » How did it feel to get the compliments?
  » How did it feel to hear them out loud?
  » What is the best way to respond to a compliment?
- Take home your compliments and add them your mirror or wall. Read them at least once a day.

❧ Closing the Session

⏱ 5 minutes

Purpose
- To provide closure for the group.
- To give feedback to the leaders.
- To explain homework activities.

Materials
- Repeat The Link (A1-6) exercise as in Session 1

Procedure
- Go over the homework assignments and ask for any questions.

Homework

📖 Readings
- True Story 2 – I Like Me (A2-1)
- Listening and Hearing (A2-2)

◎ Activities
- Try your new listening skills in real life. Do it occasionally and record your reactions in your journal.
- Complete the exercise Get to your Point (A2-6)
- Post the compliments given to them by the others in the group on their mirror in their rooms and look at them before they go to bed and first thing in the morning.
- Record any thoughts or feelings in your journal.
- Give three compliments to other people and record the results in your journal.
- Close the session with The Link exercise (A1-6) as in the first session.

Notes

Session 3
Values and Respecting Rights

Overview

☼	**Goal**	To teach participants to value their rights and those of others and consider their own values when making decisions.
✎	**Materials**	Sheets of 8-1/2" x 11" paper or cardboard with a "right" written on each, blank 8-1/2 x 11" paper or cardboard, marking pens, tape, packet of "trade-offs" for each participant, Resource Sheets A3-1 to A3-8, pencils, The Link Exercise (A1-6), diary.
⚷	**Teacher Instructions**	Homework Review Skill Instruction: My Values Discussion: Rights and Responsibilities Skill Instruction: Other People's Rights Exercise Instruction: The Swap Meet Exercise Instruction: Rights Role Play Closing the Session
📄	**Student Resource Sheets**	Activity: My Values (A3-1) Activity: Personal Rights (A3-2) Activity : Everybody Has Rights (A3-3) Activity: The Swap Meet ("Trade-offs") (A3-4) Activity Sheet: Observer's Check list (A3-5) Read: Misfits? (A3-6) Supplemental Exercise: Additional Value Suggestions (A3-7) Supplemental Exercise: Discovering Me (A3-8) Supplemental Exercise: Building Confidence (A3-9)
➠	**Homework**	Read: Misfits? (A3-6) Use "rights" won in swap meet Give three compliments to other people Continue to practice using listening skills Record in your journal: results of using rights won in swap meet; results of giving three compliments to other people; reactions from practicing listening skills; what have you learned about yourself

Homework Review

⏰ 15 minutes

Purpose
- To evaluate the understanding of concepts introduced in previous session.
- To see where further practice is needed.
- To provide positive feedback for any attempts of assertive behavior or listening skills.

Materials
- Resource Sheets A2-1 through A2-8, journal sheets (Appendix F), diary

Procedure
- Check journal entries and ask for concerns, problems, questions.
- For Get to Your Point (A2-6), go around the circle, starting on your usual side and ask each girl to give one example of a concrete response.
    - » Ask the others, what they liked about the response.
    - » Then ask if there is any other way to improve it.
    - » The leader can tell the group: "If you are talking to a person who is not being specific, you can help her by saying such things as: 'I'm not sure I understand.' 'Is that good or bad?' 'What do you mean by . . . ?' 'Can you give me an example.' "
- In a later session we will practice having conversations.
- Ask for reactions to giving compliments? How did people receive them?

Notes

❖ Skill Instruction: My Values

🕐 20 minutes

Purpose
- To have participants clarify and become conscious of their values.
- To realize how values influence decisions and when to be assertive.
- To practice publicly defending and explaining their choices.

Materials
- Resource Sheet A3-1

Procedure
- Explain what values are and their importance:
    - » "Values are your beliefs. They are important to you and you base your choices, behavior, and actions on these values. If you believe that taking care of your body and health is important, you will be able to decide whether or not to take drugs or alcohol, to exercise, and to eat healthy food."
- Turn to Resource Sheet A3-1 and have them rank order the alternatives to each item with one being of most importance.
- After completing the sheet, ask a participant to name their number one for the first item and explain why.
- Ask if anyone chose a different alternative for number one. Why? Did anyone not like any of the alternatives and might have thought of a different one?
- State, "There are no right or better answers, it's up to you!"

There are additional or alternative suggestions for forced choice values on Resource Sheet A3-7 as Additional Value Suggestions. The leaders may want to include more alternatives or select those that would be more relevant to their group.

Notes

Discussion: Rights and Responsibilities

🕐 15 minutes

Purpose
- To understand that even teenagers have rights.
- To recognize the rights of other people.
- To claim these rights in becoming assertive.
- To consider the consequences of choices.

Materials
- Resource Sheet A3-2

Discussion
- Leaders explain that teenagers often don't know how they would like to behave because they are not sure what rights they have and what rights belong to others.
- Leaders discuss rights as follows. "All persons have a basic right to be treated fairly and as a person of worth with the same rights, privileges, and responsibilities as everyone else. Rights include your values—a belief or a feeling about something that's important or worthwhile to you. For example, if you believe you have the right to be treated with respect, you will not let others treat you badly, take advantage of you, talk you into doing things you don't want to.
- The skill we will learn here—being assertive—is the way you will act in order to uphold your rights.
- Rights are not given to you, you must claim them (by your behavior).
- *But,* you must realize that other people have rights also.
- Having rights doesn't mean you can do whatever you want. Remember, the other person also has the right to express opinions, make mistakes, etc. Moreover, there are responsibilities attached to each right. For example, you have the right to make mistakes, but it's your responsibility to acknowledge your mistake, try not to make the same mistake again, and accept the fact that other people can make mistakes.
- What happens when two person's rights clash? Try to be flexible not rigid. Can some compromise be worked out? However, if your integrity—your basic beliefs—are involved, then stick to it.
- Unfortunately, there is no law that says we must be treated fairly. Often we are but let's face it, there are some mean people. What can we do about them. Try to take into consideration their situation, focus on your own goal. Perhaps your self-respect would be increased by just expressing your opinion instead of dwelling on how unfair you have been treated.
- Finally, you have to remember that as long as you live in your parent's house, allowing them to take care of your needs, your first obligation has to be to them. Almost always.

Procedure

- After discussing the above, turn to Resource Sheet A3-2 on Personal Rights and go over them. Give an example to illustrate each one.
- As homework or a conclusion to this discussion have the participants record situations where they did not act assertively. Which rights were involved?

❧ Skill Instruction: Other People's Rights

🕒 15 minutes

Purpose
- To understand that other people also have the same rights.
- To practice empathy by standing in the other person's place.

Materials
- Resource Sheet A3-3, newsprint or chalkboard, markers

Discussion
- The leaders start the discussion by saying that we've talked about our own rights now let's talk about the rights of other people we come in contact with frequently. We will look at the three scenarios on Resource Sheet A3-3 involving the three kinds of people.
- Volunteers can role play each scenario or they can be read out loud.
- After each scenario, leaders ask participants what the rights are of each person in the scenario and lists them on newsprint.

Procedure
- Let's look at the first scenario of a commercial situation with a sales clerk.
- Leaders asks for volunteers to role play the scenarios or asks someone to read them out loud.
- Leaders ask what are Andrea's rights and lists them on newsprint.
- Then leader asks what are the cashier's rights and lists them.

Scenario 1

Andrea has been waiting to give her money to the cashier after choosing the perfect tee-shirt. The cashier is chatting to a friend and seems to be ignoring Andrea. Finally Andrea has lost patience and says loudly to the cashier. "Hey, how about some service here. I've been waiting forever!"

- The next scenario is a peer situation.

Scenario 2

Cara's friend Beth is going to try smoking cigarettes and wants Cara to join her. Cara doesn't want her friend to think she's not cool but doesn't really want to. Cara says, "You shouldn't smoke, it's not healthy, it makes you stink and I'm telling you this for your own good."

- The last situation is with someone in authority.

> ## Scenario 3
>
> Hillary's dad has just told her she is grounded for a week because she came home two hours later than she had promised. Hillary says, "But it wasn't my fault, my driver didn't want to leave. You're not being fair!"

- Think of situations where you want to be assertive with the groups listed on your Resource Sheet. Write three rights these people have.
    » Commercial people (salesclerk, office workers)
    » Authority (parents, teachers, doctors, bosses)
    » Peers (friends, teenagers, persons your age, boys)

⚡ Exercise Instruction: The Swap Meet

🕐 45 minutes

Purpose

- To have participants realize that changing behavior involves risks.
- To confront the trade-offs they use that keep them nonassertive.
- To make some decisions to relinquish those they are ready to give up in favor of achieving self-respect.

Materials

- Each "right" written on a piece of 8 1/2" x 11" paper or cardboard plus some extra blank paper, tape, marking pens, Resource Sheet A3-4, scissors.

Discussion

- The leader tells participants that if they want increased control over their lives, greater self-respect, respect from others, and to be able to get along better with others, they have to give up some of the so-called benefits, known as secondary gains or "trade-offs" they got from being nonassertive.
- These trade-offs may have had some short-term usefulness to them but in the long run they resulted in being treated like a door mat, being ignored, losing friends, and feeling lousy.
- The leaders go over the different kinds of secondary gains (trade-offs) and discuss each one's short-term benefits and the long-term expenses to the participants. "For example, if I want the right to say no to some requests, I give up the trade-off of always pleasing others. But I do gain in independence, confidence choosing what I need and like, and in self-esteem."

Procedure

- Mount each "right card" on the wall so that the group can see them.
- Have the participants cut apart the secondary gains or trade-offs on the The Swap Meet Trade-Off Sheet (A3-4).
- Ask the participants to focus on three or four of the "rights" posted on the wall that they would really like to own (ones they do not already have).
- Now have them arrange their trade-offs into three piles—one pile they can give up fairly easily, a second pile consisting of pay-offs that are somewhat harder to give up, and possibly a third pile that may be difficult or impossible to do without.
- Start the bargaining by saying, "These rights are all for sale. Which right do you want? Let's start the bargaining. How many trade-offs are you willing to give me for it and what are they? Who else wants this right? Will you give me more trade-offs than the last bidder?" (The bidders do not have to give up identical trade-offs.)

- The first bargainer tells what trade-off she is paying for the right. If others are bidding on the same right, they need only tell about the additional trade-offs that are different.
- Help bidders realize what they are giving up by questioning them about the meaning the trade-offs and the rights have for them.
- Give the posted right to the highest bidder to keep. If there is a tie, give them both the right.

◆ Exercise Instruction: Rights Role Play

⏲ 45 minutes

Purpose
- To allow participants to practice using the rights won in the swap meet.
- To try the first step in changing behavior before using their rights in the real world.

Materials
- Resource Sheet A3-5

Discussion
- Since this is the group's first experience with role-playing, the leaders will model a role-playing situation first.
- Leaders choose a right they would like to own (leaders are not perfect either) and decide on a situation that gives them difficulty, such as a commercial transaction, work situation, or one dealing with social or authority figures.
- Choose someone from your group or your co-leader to role play the situation with you.
- Do not play the situation assertively, but rather how you usually do it.
- Ask the group for feedback first, what they thought was assertive, then what they thought needed improvement.
- Have them use Resource Sheet A3-5 as a guide.
- Ask the co-leader for feedback, thus modeling appropriate procedure.
- Using the feedback, role play the situation again, this time assertively.
- Again ask for feedback.

Procedure
- Divide the participants into groups of three. Ask each participant to think of a not very scary situation for practicing the right they won at the swap meet.
- Have each group decide on an asserter, a responder, and an observer. Tell them they will each take a turn at every role.
- The asserter briefly tells the responder about the situation and the role the responder is to play. Asserters should not waste time talking about the situation but should concentrate on explaining the situation briefly and concretely and moving on to practice the behavior.
- The role play should focus the message on what the participants feel and/or what they want, for example, "I feel annoyed when I try to study with the TV going full blast, please turn it down!"
- The *responder* reacts normally, as if they were the person in the situation, If they feel like defending themselves by giving excuses, acting guilty or angry in response to the asserter's attempts, they should act that way.

- The *observer,* using the observer's check list as a guide, checks the behavior of the asserter and write suggestions to use as feedback.

✑ Closing the Session

⏲ 5 minutes

Purpose
- To provide closure for the group.
- To give feedback to the leaders.
- To explain homework activities.

Materials
- Resource Sheet A3-6, The Link (A1-6) from Session 1

Homework
📖 Reading
- Misfits? (A3-6)

◎ Activities
- Use "rights" won in swap meet
- Give three compliments to different people
- Continue practice using listening skills
- Record in your journal: results of using rights won in swap meet; results of giving three compliments to different people; reactions from practicing listening skills; have you learned something about yourself
- Close the session with The Link exercise (A1-6)

Notes

Session 4
Blocks to Assertion

Overview

Goal
To develop strategies for decreasing stress by learning how thoughts can influence feelings and replacing negative mental messages with positive ones.

Materials
Resource Sheets A4-1 through A4-8, newsprint, markers, a small flat stone for each girl, dairy.

Teacher Instructions
Homework Review
Exercise Instruction: What This Session is About
Skill Exercise: Stop That Thought!
Exercise Instruction: Bad News Beliefs
Exercise Instruction: Bad News, Good News
Skill Exercise: Stopping My Bad News Voice
Skill Exercise: Finding My Magnificent True Self
Closing the Session
Supplemental Instruction: Take a Deep Breath

Student Resource Sheets
Blocks to Assertion (A4-1)
Bad News Beliefs (A4-2)
Bad News, Good News (A4-3)
Stopping My Bad News Voice (A4-4)
True Story 3 – Early Warning Signals (A4-5)
My True Self (A4-6)
Supplemental Exercise: Getting Rid of Toxic Waste (A4-7)
Supplemental Exercise: Learning to Listen to Your Early Warning Signals (A4-8)

Homework
Read True Story 3 – Early Warning Signals (A4-5)
My True Self (A4-6) – find a stone or choose an object as a symbol and paint or decorate that object
Record your responses to the following activities in your journal: practice imagining a stressful situation and using your good news beliefs (accurate plus positive statements) to calm your stressful feelings, 10 minutes each day; give two compliments, one to a friend, one to a parent; notice if someone gives you a compliment

Homework Review

🕐 15 Minutes

Purpose

- To evaluate the understanding of the concepts introduced in the previous session.
- To see if further practice is needed.
- To provide positive feedback for successful movement toward assertive behavior.

Materials

- Resource Sheets A3-1 through A3-9, last session's journal sheets, diary

Procedure

- Check journal sheets.
- Leaders ask for reactions to participants when they attempted to use their rights.
- Compliment the slightest action, even if it is just an awareness that they had this right, whether or not they acted on it. There is a whole gamut of success, all are to be encouraged.
- If they are unhappy with their behavior or if they didn't know what to do ask, "What would you have liked to have happened," then "What would you have liked to have said." This is usually an assertive response and verbalizing now will give them the words to use next time. (No swear words allowed.)
- If it is an aggressive response, ask them what rights the other person has. Then with that in mind, is there another way to say what they want.
- Ask the others in the group for suggestions on how they would respond assertively.
- What happened when they gave or received compliments?

Notes

❦ Skill Exercise: What This Session Is About

🕒 5 minutes

Purpose
- To explain focus of this session.
- To become aware of thinking patterns that lead to ineffectual behaviors.
- To reduce stress and anxiety in certain personal situations.
- To increase a memory bank of effective responses for that situation.
- To recognize unrealistic assumptions and catastrophizing and replace these with realistic possibilities.

Materials
- Newsprint posted on the wall with the following message found on Resource Sheet A4-1:

Blocks to Assertion

We do not believe we have the right.

We do not want to take the responsibility.

We use unrealistic beliefs or fears.

We lack the skills.

Discussion
- The leaders discuss the following: The blocks to being assertive are related. If we do not believe we have the *right*, we will not take the *responsibility* for speaking out, following through with our opinions or our feelings. If we *fear* loss of approval, affection, hurting others, looking stupid, or being selfish we don't develop the *skills* to communicate our assertive message.
- We often use unrealistic assumptions or mistaken beliefs that keep us from being strong and ourselves.
- Since we believe all these things, we have never developed the skills or practiced them so that we can become stronger and more in control of our lives.
- Today we are going to work on how to recognize these mistaken beliefs and become more realistic in our thinking. You will find out that when you do this you will become less fearful in scary situations and able to handle yourselves better.
- What you will gain is respect from other people. Not everybody will love you but they will respect you. Girl power!

- How did these beliefs start? Probably when you were a little kid and some grown-up with the best intentions in the world said "How dare you talk back to me, children should be seen, not heard," Or in a moment of irritation, "you're just too lazy for words." Or kids on the block called you "stupid" or said "that's a stupid thing to say."

☙ Skill Exercise: Stop That Thought!

⏲ 10 Minutes

Purpose
- To realize the relationship between thinking and feeling.
- To practice how feelings can be controlled by changing your thinking.

Procedure
- Divide the participants into pairs picking a person they have not been with before.
- Ask each person to silently think about some disturbing experience or coming event they will face in the near future that causes them anxiety or anger. Do they have to give a report in front of the class. Are they in a play? Are they applying for a job? Is there something they must tell their mom or dad?
- Give them a few minutes to imagine the situation and to let the feeling build up.
- Suddenly shout "Stop!"
- Ask the group, what happened to their thoughts.
- When the participants report that their thoughts went away, discuss how they can influence their thoughts. They can tell themselves "Stop!" Then replace those fearful thoughts with some accurate, realistic, positive thoughts.
- Now the leaders say, "Now start your stream of negative thoughts again, the same ones you used to scare yourself the first time. This time, you say "Stop!" out loud. Replace your negative thoughts with positive thoughts until your panic lessens. Examples could be: "I've done this before and survived." "What's the worst that could happen? I'm not going to die." Use whatever statements that will help you."
- Have them tell their positive statements to their partner.
- Ask the participants to start their negative thoughts again, but this time ask them to yell "Stop" silently and repeat their coping thoughts to themselves.

Discussion
- Discuss how the "stop" technique worked in the group as a whole. Ask what happened to their negative thoughts. Ask how their feelings changed. Warn them that this technique is only to demonstrate that negative thoughts *can* be controlled. The "stop" technique is just a stop-gap measure. During this session we will practice more effective techniques.

Notes

◆ Exercise Instruction: Bad News Beliefs

⏱ 20 minutes

Purpose
- To become aware of self-defeating thoughts.
- To learn how to replace negative thoughts with positive ones.
- To feel in control of thoughts and feeling.

Materials
- Resource Sheet A4-2, newsprint, markers

Discussion
- Leaders turn to Resource Sheet A4-2 and either read it aloud or ask different girls to read each paragraph. Ask them if they have ever felt this way or believe these things.
- Discuss how having the following beliefs will cause them to feel bad: having to be loved by everyone (if I don't have sex with him, he will get a different girl; if I don't drink, they won't think I'm cool), never making mistakes, having things go your way all the time.
- The good news is that we have the power to replace the bad beliefs with good ones and you will see that this will actually change your feelings.

Procedure
- Tell participants:
  » Close eyes. Remember a time when you made a mistake or felt bad about something. When you tried to practice your right, did you have any feelings of fear? Put yourself there and really feel it. Imagine the place where this happened. Was another person involved? What did he or she say? What did you say? Notice what your body feels like. What does your heart feel like? Your belly? Your chest? Now notice what you are thinking or telling yourself. Imagine that you can talk to your belly, etc. and it can talk back to you.
  » What is it saying to you? It will tell you which Bad News Belief you are buying into. What were you saying to yourself? Was it "I will lose a friend," or "I will be misunderstood," or perhaps "I will look foolish.?"
  » Now, keeping your eyes closed, make yourself feel better by thinking other thoughts until you feel more calm and peaceful. Maybe you can tell yourself, "What's the worst thing that can happen?" or "Can I live with that?" How about, "How do I know it is really true?" "Nobody's perfect, we all make mistakes. Besides nobody likes people who are right all the time."
- Wait quietly until the group looks more relaxed and calm and then ask them to open their eyes. Ask them what they said to themselves that made them feel horrible and list them on the newsprint under Bad News Beliefs.

- Next ask them to tell what they said to themselves that made them feel better and list them on another sheet—the Good News Beliefs.
- Tell them that if they had any trouble finding thoughts that would help them feel better, perhaps some on the list of Good News Beliefs would be helpful to them. Have them write down a few they think would help in their journals.
- Conclude with:
    » I'm going to treat you to a piece of bumper sticker wisdom: Don't believe everything that you think. I'll say that again don't believe everything that you think. In fact, don't believe everything you are told, don't believe everything you read. Just entertain possibilities and good ideas. Beliefs are finished and stuck information. Possibilities and good ideas can always be modified with new information as you grow and learn new things.

✺ Exercise Instruction: Bad News, Good News

🕒 20 minutes

Purpose
- To distinguish judgments from fact.
- To use the facts as a tool for replacing Bad News Beliefs with realistic statements.
- To learn to use realistic statements to substitute for negative thoughts.
- To feel in control of feelings.

Materials
- Resource Sheet A4-3

Discussion
- Discuss as follows:
  » Remember what we read about Bad News Beliefs (BNB)? Thoughts like "That was a stupid thing to say," "No one will like me because I'm ugly," "They won't like me unless I agree with them," "I'm not cool unless I have the right clothes," are all Bad News Beliefs. They are all put downs to your basic self, which is love itself.
  » They are all based on judgments, not facts. So what's the difference between a judgment and a fact? A fact is based on observation. It is neither good nor bad. It is objective. A judgment is one step removed from fact. It is emotional. It is changeable depending on the value system. For example: **Fact:** Joey killed 10 men with a semi-automatic. **Judgment**: He is a murderer. Or **Judgment:** He is a war hero. **Fact**: I weigh 117 pounds. **Judgment**: I am too fat (to fit into the size 3 jeans I wore in high school) or I am too skinny (to fit into the size 9s my friend gave me.)

Procedure
- Go over instructions on Resource Sheet A4-3.
- After the participants write their factual statements, ask them if it changed their feelings.
- How did their feelings change when they added a positive statement?
- Now have them shut their eyes and imagine themselves thinking about one of the BNBs they worked on. Let themselves allow their feelings to escalate.
- Next, with eyes still closed, have them slide to their factual statement and then to their positive statement.
- Ask "what happened to their feelings."

Notes

⊷ Skill Exercise: Stopping My Bad News Voice*

🕒 15 minutes

Purpose
- To teach participants another skill to help stop negative messages.
- To learn to resist peer pressure.
- To build self-esteem.

Materials
- Resource Sheet A4-4

Discussion
- The leader introduces the skill activity by telling the participants that another way or an additional help to stop Bad News Beliefs and replace them with Good News Beliefs is to say "Thank you for sharing but," whenever they hear that voice in their head telling them bad things just as if they were responding to a real person who is trying to put you down.
- They should also give that voice a name. Examples: "Critic," "Judge," or even a real name like "Susan" or "Betty."
- Now when their bad news voice starts to tell them things like "I'm not smart enough," or "I'll have no friends," or "They won't like me," they can stop that voice with words like "I'm sorry you feel that way, Critic, but that's not true, I am a good person and have other friends," or whatever positive Good News Beliefs you have thought of before.
- Tell participants this a good way to handle put-downs and peer pressure also.

Procedure
- Ask everyone to think of a name for their bad news voice and write it on their activity sheet.
- Next pair up with a partner you have not been with before.
- One of the pair should act as the bad news voice saying things that are put-downs.
- The other partner responds with a positive statement using the name they have given their bad news voice. Example: Bad news voice: "You look a mess," or "You're a wimp for not going." Good news voice: "I'm sorry you feel that way, Critic, but the truth is I have good reasons for not going along with you."
- The person role-playing the bad news voice gives three or four put-downs with the other partner responding each time with their bad news name and a positive statement.

---

*Adapted from *Group Exercises for Enhancing Social Skills and Self-Esteem* (Vol. 2, pp. 75 and 77, Exercise 35–Changing My Critical Inner Voice), by S. S. Khalsa, 1999, Sarasota, Fla.: Professional Resource Press, P. O. Box 15560, Sarasota, FL 34277-1560. Copyright 1999 by Professional Resource Exchange, Inc. Adapted with permission.

- Have partners change roles after three or four criticisms.
- Ask the group how effective was this method and whether or not it worked for them.

Notes

✥ Skill Exercise: Finding My Magnificent True Self

🕒 45 minutes

Purpose
- To raise self-esteem
- To introduce participants to their inner resources.
- To demonstrate that self-worth, guidance, nurturance, and personal truth come from within.
- To teach participants how to trust themselves.
- To learn how to relax and relieve stress.

Materials
- Blankets and pillows (optional), pencils, personal journals

Procedure
- The leader instructs the participants to find comfortable positions, dims lights, if possible.
- The leader reads the visualization exercise out loud in a gentle, slow, warm, lulling voice.
- At the end of the process, the leader raises the lights again and instructs the participants to write for five to 10 minutes in their journals about their experience.
- Writing should be followed by a short bathroom break and a discussion.

Procedure

The leader reads in a gentle, low, lulling voice:

Just begin by finding a comfortable position. If you want you can lie down on the floor, or sit on the floor with your back leaning against a wall. Let yourself move around however you like until you feel really comfortable . . . and when you do . . . you can just allow your eyes to close . . . and maybe take a nice big . . . deep . . . breath . . . (pause for one full inhalation and exhalation). Then on the next in breath continue breathing in deeply . . . and then letting the air out . . . in a b-i-i-i-g sigh. (Take a deep breath and sigh "Ahhhhhhhhh"). You can even pretend that you have an extra set of nostrils in the bottoms of your feet . . . and when you breathe . . . you can imagine . . . inhaling from the bottoms of your feet . . . all the way up your legs . . . through your stomach . . . and up into your lungs . . . and then exhaling any fidgets right out . . . through the bottoms of your feet . . . (longer pause).

Good. Just begin to become aware of your body . . . resting . . . just as it is . . . and as you do . . . you can become aware . . . of where the floor . . . or wall . . . or chair . . . or blanket . . . is touching your skin . . . and where it isn't . . . (longer pause), how the floor . . . or chair or wall . . . is supporting you . . . holding you up . . . without you doing anything at all . . . now your breath goes in . . . and out . . . on its own . . . (pause) . . . you can feel your breath . . . coming into your chest . . . and going out . . . You can . . . hear the sound of my voice . . . without having to do anything . . . it just happens by itself . . . naturally and easily . . . making it easier and easier for you to . . . unwind a little more . . . into a soft and easy comfortable feeling.

Just imagine now . . . that you are . . . walking down a beautiful path . . . Maybe this path is in a beautiful meadow or park . . . or in the mountains somewhere . . . or along a beach . . . or even in a fairy-tale land . . . just let whatever feels right for you to . . . form in your imagination (pause).

Perhaps you can feel . . . or see . . . or sense yourself . . . walking down this path . . . wearing whatever you want to imagine yourself wearing . . . (pause) walking along . . . noticing how beautiful it is . . . Maybe there are beautiful flowers . . . or trees along the path . . . maybe you can hear birds singing . . . feel a soft breeze in your hair . . . feel the warm gentle light of the sun on your face . . . It's a beautiful day . . . and you have all . . . the . . . time . . . in . . . the . . . world . . .

As you look down the path . . . you might begin to notice . . . a beautiful rainbow forming in front of you (pause). The interesting thing about this rainbow . . . is . . . that it stays where it is . . . as you move closer . . . The closer you get . . . the more beautiful it gets . . . You may even begin to feel . . . the gentle magical sparkliness of the colors . . . as you approach . . .

Soon . . . you get close enough to . . . step right into the rainbow, now . . . and as you do . . . you can . . . feel the magic . . . of the rainbow . . . as you . . . drift . . . into a soft and warm feeling . . . of comfort . . . peace . . . and happiness . . . (pause). Pretty soon . . . you notice . . . that there are some colorful steps going up into the rainbow . . . and as you step up . . . onto the first step . . . you can feel the color red . . . gently filling your body . . . and surrounding you with love . . . safety . . . and protection (pause).

Then as you step up to the next step . . . you can allow yourself to . . . feel the color orange surrounding you . . . and filling you with a light and happy feeling . . . (pause). Then, the next step . . . Yellow . . . You are surrounded and filled with . . . the joyful . . . peaceful color of sunshine yellow (pause). Then the next step: Green (pause). Just allow yourself to . . . be filled and surrounded with the soothing color of green (pause). Then you step . . . on the next step . . . blue (pause). And you can feel yourself . . . surrounded and filled . . . with the wonderful color of blue

(pause). It forms almost like a . . . bubble of safety . . . love . . . and protection . . . all around you (pause). Then the last step . . . purple . . . And you let the beautiful . . . magnificent . . . color of purple surround you and fill you . . . with even more love . . .

And there you are . . . standing in front of a very special door (pause). Just allow yourself to . . . imagine this beautiful door to your special place . . . your inner safe place . . . Your place of play . . . and love . . . peace and specialness . . . Your place of magic . . . and connection . . . to your heart . . . and to your true magnificent self (pause).

So imagine this door now . . . (pause). It may be a door of light . . . or color . . . that only you can see . . . Or an ancient . . . carved golden door . . . that only you can find . . . Have it be any way that feels right to you . . . (pause). And notice that . . . when you are ready . . . this special door recognizes you . . . and only you . . . and begins to open for you. Just allow yourself to . . . move through the doorway . . . into this very . . . special . . . place that is yours . . . and yours alone . . . Let it be however it feels right for you . . . Notice . . . just how good it feels to be here . . . Notice whatever special things are here . . . the furniture . . . if there is furniture . . . Or maybe it is a special outdoors kind of place with soft grass . . . Or the inside of a magical castle . . . or . . . whatever is right for you . . . Make it just the way you want it to be . . . (longer pause) . . . And as you stand there . . . noticing what this place is like . . . for you . . . you can . . . just imagine . . . a beautiful white light . . . beginning to shine down on you . . . filling you with light . . . and washing away any negativity or problems from your life . . . until you feel pure . . . and clear . . . and refreshed . . . and free.

And then . . . when you're ready . . . you can begin to . . . move into the main room . . . of your special place . . . and find a very comfortable place to sit . . . or lie down (pause). Maybe its a very cushy couch . . . or bed covered with velvet cushions . . . let it be just the way you want it . . . If you like . . . you can invite your favorite animal . . . or pet . . . to be here with you . . . as you . . . get even more comfortable . . . and maybe even see yourself . . . closing your eyes . . . feeling so happy . . . safe . . . and peaceful . . . (pause).

Just begin to . . . become aware of your heart (pause). Your heart . . . is a very special place inside you . . . where all of your love . . . and magic . . . and all the answers . . . to all of your questions lives (pause). It is also where your magnificent true self lives . . . Just imagine that you are putting your hand over your heart . . . and as you imagine . . . putting your hand over your heart . . . you can . . . begin to . . . feel it filling up with a radiant . . . golden sun . . . of light and love . . .

And . . . as you . . . feel that . . . radiant light . . . filling your heart . . . just allow the warm golden feeling in your heart to . . . grow stronger . . . and fuller . . . and more sparkly . . . just . . . filling you . . . with golden light (pause). You can allow this golden light . . . to fill you completely . . . preparing you to meet your . . . magnificent . . . radiant . . . true self.

Take a deep breath in . . . and as you exhale . . . you can begin to imagine . . . feel . . . sense . . . a beautiful white light . . . forming . . . in the middle of your special place (pause). Maybe . . . at first . . . this white light . . . begins to take the shape of a beautiful star (pause). Then . . . maybe . . . you can . . . begin to see or sense . . . a beautiful figure . . . standing inside the star (pause). Just allow yourself to . . . watch the figure become clearer and clearer . . . until . . . you can really sense . . . see . . . experience . . . this beautiful being . . . in the star . . . (pause). Perhaps . . . this beautiful self . . . looks just like you . . . but maybe just a little older . . . more grown up . . . wiser . . . more confident . . . self-assured . . . graceful . . . full of love . . . for herself . . . for you . . . for all the creatures of the world . . . (pause). This splendid being . . . knows you . . . understands you . . . and loves you . . . just the way you are (pause). This magnificent being . . . is your inside — you —your magnificent true inner radiant self . . . (pause) and now . . . you can meet her . . . feel her love . . . and get to know her.

Go ahead and allow yourself to . . . move closer to her . . . (pause). Say hello . . . feel her love . . . wisdom . . . and strength . . . (pause). She may have something to tell you . . . or show you . . . let that happen now . . . (longer pause).

You may have a question you would like to ask her. Go ahead and ask your question . . . (pause) . . . and just allow the answer to come to you now . . . (longer pause). Think of something you would like her to help you with (longer pause) . . . ask her to help you now . . . (pause) and . . . allow her to . . . show you a picture of you . . . getting all the help you need . . . from the inside . . . from inside your heart . . . and you can allow yourself to . . . see yourself . . . doing whatever it is . . . beautifully . . . and well . . . feeling good about yourself . . . and everyone around you.

I am going to be quiet for just a few minutes now . . . to allow you to . . . spend more time with your magnificent true self. You may take the time to . . . ask her questions . . . or to just feel her love . . . you may want to ask her to hold you . . . or show you positive pictures of your future happiness . . . Just let whatever feels right to you . . . to happen . . . now . . . (pause for two minutes).

Good (pause). You may now . . . if you like . . . ask your True Magnificent Self . . . for a name that you can call her . . . Just let a name come to you now . . . the first name that comes to mind is okay... (pause). Good (pause). She would like to give you a gift... a picture or maybe something symbolic... (pause) to take back with you... (pause). Allow yourself to receive it. Now... (pause) spend a few moments with this gift... noticing what it means to you... (longer pause). Now, if it feels right to you... go ahead and hug her... and thank her for being with you... (pause).

Then... just allow her to... blend back into the light... of the star... she first appeared in... And... as that happens... you can... just allow that star to... enter into your heart... (pause).

Feel it there... in your heart... Radiating love and light... confidence... strength... and happiness... (pause). Then let the light... spread throughout your entire body... filling your whole body... from the top of your head... to the tips of your toes... with light... love... confidence... and happiness.

Go ahead and... quietly, inside yourself... say her name... feel the light and love... say her name again... So now... you know... anytime you wish to... feel her presence inside of you... all you have to do is... say her name... and feel her filling you up with love... light... confidence... strength and happiness (pause). Good.

Now... in a moment... you are going to leave your special place... knowing that you can return... any time you want... all you need to do is... close your eyes... imagine yourself entering the rainbow... and go up the colored steps to the magical door (pause). So feel yourself now... moving towards that door... and through it... back... into the rainbow... first feeling the color purple as you step down (pause). Then blue (pause and go slowly). Then green... feeling the color green all around and through you. Then yellow... Feel the color yellow. Then... orange... letting it go all around you. And then... red... feeling the color red... And then... allow yourself to... step out of the rainbow... back on to the path (pause).

See... feel... imagine yourself coming back up the path... past the butterfly you saw earlier... And... taking your time now... gently bringing yourself... back to this room... becoming aware of your body now... resting... just as it is... (pause).

Go ahead and take a nice... deep... full... breath... (pause). Go ahead and begin to... wiggle your fingers and toes... stretch... (pause). Go ahead and stretch your arms up, over your head, taking a nice deep full breath... getting ready to open your eyes... you can take your time... and when you feel ready... just open your eyes (wait for every one to open their eyes). Good!

Discussion

After the visualization exercise the leader asks the girls to share significant aspects of their experience with the group. Some possible questions are:

- What is your special place like?
- What did your magnificent true self look like? How did it feel to be with her?
- Do any of you wish to share the questions you asked and the answers you received?
- What did you learn about yourself?
- What kind of gift did you receive? What does it mean to you?
- What did you like the most about this inner journey?
- Ask them what they experienced during this exercise.
- Then have them write about what they experienced in their journals and if there is time have them draw the gift or symbol they received either on a special stone or some other object.
- Otherwise have them decorate their stone or other object as homework.
- This exercise can also be used as a relaxation exercise with the visualizations useful in relieving stress.

Closing the Session

⏲ 5 minutes

Purpose
- To provide closure for the group
- To give feedback to the leaders
- To explain homework activities

Materials
- Resource Sheets A4-5 and A4-6, The Link (A1-6) on newsprint, journal

Homework
📖 Reading
- True Story 4 – Early Warning Signals (A4-5).

◎ Activities
- Discuss homework exercises.
- Find a stone or object and paint or decorate it with a symbol—flower, sun, or whatever—to illustrate your true self. Keep it in your pocket or somewhere on your person so you will always have it with you as a reminder. Perhaps it will look different to you at the end of each day, depending on how you feel about yourself.
- Record your responses to the following activities in your journal: practice imagining a stressful situation and using your Good News Beliefs (accurate plus positive statements) to calm your stressful feelings, 10 minutes each day.
- Give two compliments, one to a friend, one to a parent; notice if someone gives you a compliment.
- Call on your magnificent true self whenever you need her.
- Close the session with The Link (A1-6) as in the first session.

Notes

❧ Supplemental Instruction: Take a Deep Breath

Purpose
- To learn another quick strategy for handling stress.
- To increase stress releasing habits.

Discussion
- The leader explains that this is another version of the "stop" exercise, or of the strategy of counting to 10 when you are upset.
- This gives you a chance to cool down while you decide what to do.
- It is also another way to clear your mind of the BNBs so that you can replace them with good news or positive thoughts.
- This is based on the relationship between the body, mind and breath. Breathing in, holding your breath, and telling yourself relax while you breath out, helps to clear the mind and relax the body.

Procedure
- Participants can be paired up or can practice individually.
- Ask participants to think of a stressful situation that they may be facing soon.
- After a minute say, "Inhale slowly and then hold your breath at the end of the inhalation. Then exhale slowly while you say to yourself "relax."
- Ask the participants what happened to their thoughts when they held their breath. How do they feel afterward.
- This exercise can be used whenever they are feeling angry or frustrated also. Practicing it often can even help them from getting angry or frustrated in the first place.

Session 5
Learning to Say "No"

Overview

Goal — To learn and practice specific skills in refusing requests, resisting manipulation, and the value of persistence

Materials — Newsprint, marking pens, Resource Sheets A5-1 through A5-7, The Link (A1-6) on newsprint, dairy.

Teacher Instructions —
Homework Review
Discussion: Peer Pressure
Skill Instruction: Handling Peer Pressure
Skill Instruction: Give Me Some Space
Skill Instruction: Refusing Requests
Skill Instruction: Role Playing Saying "No"
Skill Instruction: Combining Persistence with Understanding and a Workable Compromise
Supplemental Instruction: Negotiating a Workable Compromise
Closing the Session

Student Resource Sheets —
Activity Sheet: Peer Pressure (A5-1)
Activity Sheet: I'm In Control (A5-2)
Activity Sheet: Combining Broken Record with Understanding and a Workable Compromise (A5-3)
True Stories 4 (A5-4)
Helpful Hints for Saying "No" to Unfair Requests and Demands (A5-5)
Supplemental Exercise: Negotiating or Reaching a Workable Compromise (A5-6)
Supplemental Exercise: Keeping the Peace (A5-7)

Homework —
Read True Stories 4 (A5-4)
Read Helpful Hints for Saying "No" to Unfair Requests and Demands (A5-5)
In your journal record your reactions to the following activities: practice refusing unreasonable requests; become aware of how you handle criticism; how did you handle the compliments you receive; pay two compliments and record how they were given and received; how your "true-self" object is doing; write about your own true self and bring it to the next session to share if you wish
Supplemental Exercises: Negotiating a Workable Compromise (A5-6)
Supplemental Exercises: Keeping the Peace to (A5-7)

Homework Review

 (15 minutes)

Purpose

- To evaluate their understanding of the concepts introduced in the previous session.
- To clarify any misunderstandings
- To provide positive feedback and recognize growing self-esteem.

Materials

- Girls should have their journals, Resource Sheets A4-1 through A4-7, their homework, and their "true-self" stone or object, diary.

Procedure

- Discuss the reading on Resource Sheet A4-5 as follows:
  - Have any of you had any warning signals when you were in an uncomfortable situation?
  - What were they, how did they feel?
  - Did you have the signals before the event occurred?
  - If you had listened to the signal, what could you have done differently?
  - How can you use this information in the future?
- If there is time, the leader might have them visualize the situation as described in the supplemental exercise (A4-8) to revive the feelings and finish with the above questions.
- Go over journals to find out reactions to relaxation and stress-reducing practice.
- Did using their Good News Beliefs work.
- What worked best? What was least helpful?
- Have each girl show their "true-self" stone and say whether it seems to be shining brightly because they are pleased with how they handled themselves during the week or whether it is sort of dull because something didn't go right.
- How did they do on giving and receiving compliments?

Notes

Discussion: Peer Pressure

⏲ 10 Minutes

Purpose
- To learn the meaning of peer pressure.
- To identify types of peers each individual faces.
- To realize the relationship between peer pressure and values.

Materials
- Resource Sheet A5-1, pens or pencils.

Discussion

Review the definition of peer—"boys and girls their own age."

- Talk about the pressure they get from this age group—from boys, from girls—especially negative pressure. Negative pressure is related to antisocial behavior.
- Examples:
  » cutting school
  » shoplifting
  » having sex
  » taking drugs
  » drinking
  » smoking
- Tell the group, "Being able to resist peer pressure depends on your knowing what's important to you, deciding what you want to do, learning how to say "no," and sticking to your decision. That's what we are going to learn this session."

Procedure
- Turn to the peer-pressure activity on Resource Sheet A5-1.
- Ask each participant to list the possible negative pressures they feel from each group in the different situations.
- After about five minutes ask each girl to read aloud one negative pressure.
- If this is something the others feel but didn't think of, they should write it on their sheet.
- Have each one decide on one negative peer pressure to work on in the next activity.

Skill Instruction: Handling Peer Pressure

⏰ 10 minutes

Purpose
- To develop decision-making skills.
- To feel in control.
- To increase self-esteem.

Materials
- Resource Sheets A5-1 and A5-2, blank sheets of newsprint or chalk board with the following statements written on it.

☑ Why does this make you feel uncomfortable, what is your value or belief?
☑ What could be the consequences?
☑ This is what I choose to do instead for my best welfare.
☑ This is what I will tell them.
☑ **I will stick to my decision.**

Discussion

The leader reminds participants of the values and what they learned about them in a previous session—a personal belief or feeling about something that's important to the person. Each person's values may be different from another's. For example, one person may feel it is important not to eat meat or may believe in recycling.

Procedure
- Ask participants to choose one peer-pressure situation from the previous resource sheet (A5-1) and work on that situation on Resource Sheet A5-2.
- Ask them to write the personal belief or value that makes this situation uncomfortable for them.
- Next, based on this value, have them decide on a possible course of action based on the above statements written on newsprint or chalkboard.
- Then, write down why they choose it.
- The next activities after everyone completes this will be learning the skill to say "no" and learning the skill of sticking to your decision.

Notes

Skill Instruction: Give Me Some Space

⏰ 15 minutes

Purpose
- To help participants act assertively in situations where they are unsure of what they think or what they wanted to do.
- To practice using a suitable phrase until it becomes an automatic reply.

Materials
- Newsprint, markers

Discussion
- Leaders introduce this exercise by saying, "Being able to choose the time, the place, and the person for an assertive action is half the battle.
- Too often, however, people make requests or ask our opinions before we know what we think or what we know we want to do.
- Most of us for some reason, feel we have to reply instantly, even though we are confused, surprised, or just plain ignorant.
- Usually we answer in one of two ways; we blurt out an opinion we regret as soon as its out of our mouths, or with an awkward period of hemming and hawing. In either case, we feel we should have responded better and could kick ourselves.
- If you do not know what you think or want to do, the assertive way to handle this is to say you are uncertain and ask for more time to consider the request or question.

Procedure
- Ask the group what are some phrases they could use to give them time to think about how they want to reply and list on newsprint.
- To get them started you might suggest, "I'm not sure, I need to think about that," and "I'm not sure, let me get back to you."
- Go over the list and weed out the ones they agree are not assertive.
- Ask each girl to pick the phrase they feel most comfortable using.
- Divide the group into pairs.
- Leaders demonstrate.
- Ask one person in each pair to make about five requests requiring a response (not "How are you?"). Some examples are:
  » Would you lend me your sweater (or car)?
  » How about a movie tonight?
  » Do you want to do a sleep-over?
  » Can I come over?

> What do you think of the principal?
- Ask the second person to imagine herself responding assertively with the phrase they chose. Then have her say that and only that to every single question.
- Have participants reverse roles and repeat the steps above.
- Ask for feedback. "How did it work."
- Sometimes just the time it takes to say the phrase is enough time to decide what you want to say or do.

✂ Skill Instruction: Refusing Requests Persistence—The Broken Record or Cracked CD

🕐 30 minutes

Purpose
- To realize the effectiveness of persistence.
- To learn to recognize manipulation and develop skills to counter it.

Materials
- Completed resource sheets (A5-1 and A5-2) from the previous exercises.

Discussion
- Discuss the concept of persistence with the group as follows:
    » Nonassertive persons become easily frustrated and allow themselves to be manipulated or talked into things, giving up their rights. Because of their frustration, they back down at the first sign of what they see as conflict. As a result, nonassertive persons teach others that they can be talked into anything. These are the girls that are preyed on by certain kinds of boys. These are the girls who are on the "can't say no" lists whenever all kinds of help and dirty work is needed. It is helpful to recognize when you are being manipulated and be able to resist this.
- Manipulative people use these approaches:
    » Asking for reasons. "Why" questions trap you into long, involved explanations that can be opposed.
    » Logic: This works if you have the same goal, but most people in conflict do not. The other person overwhelms you with the reasonableness of his or her requests.
    » Answers: You are made to feel you should always have a ready answer. If you do not, then you must cave in to the requests. (Don't forget about saying, "I need to think about that.")
    » Problems: The manipulator says, "We have a problem." Since many of us like to be helpful, we become involved in helping the other person solve his or her problem.
    » Understanding. It is expected that you should understand without having to be told.
    » Caring. You are told, "If you really cared you would do this."
    » You are told you should never change your mind. "You did it before," or "You said you would yesterday." (Remember your rights.)
    » Guilt. "I helped you before."
    » Changing the subject. "Of course, you can go. That reminds me, Brandon wants to know what we think of his new tattoo."
    » Helplessness. "I'm not good at this. I've never done it before."
- Remember:
    » You do not have to have reasons.

- » You do not have to have answers.
- » You do not have to have solutions to other people's problems.
- Why do you use the broken-record technique to be persistent?
  - » To make a request when the other person is extremely aggressive or manipulative.
  - » To refuse a request when the other person is discounting, manipulative, or destructive.
  - » To prevent someone from manipulating you.
  - » To settle a conflict on the real issues.
  - » To make sure the other person hears your opinions.
- How do you use the broken-record technique?
  - » Keep saying what you want to say over and over again. Repeat your point in a matter-of-fact but firm way.
  - » Stick to your point. You can let the other person know that you understand his or her position, but you ignore side issues and personal attacks. Respond to legitimate points and perhaps give a brief explanation of your position.
  - » Keep repeating what you want until your request is met, or until your request is denied and all possible alternatives have been explored.
    - ○ Repeating your point to the extreme is only appropriate when the other person is extremely aggressive destructive, manipulative, or disregarding. For example, consider a situation where a mother completely ignores everything her daughter says. Finally the daughter says in a voice loud enough to overshadow her mother's, "I've heard the same criticism over and over. It hurts me. Please, I've heard you and I don't want to hear it any more, let's move on." Parts of this statement may have to be repeated many times before the mother stops long enough to hear what her daughter wants to say.
  - » What if the other person is also assertive and is persistent?
    - ○ Fine. Everyone should be assertive. You will settle differences between you and the other person by reaching a workable compromise, not by one person manipulating the other.
  - » Caution: Don't forget, there may a situation in which it is not realistic to be assertive—the consequences may be too unpleasant or disastrous. These situations usually involve differences in power (such as between employer and worker, and even between parent and child). In these situations, you may want to accept compromises that you would not otherwise accept. On the other hand, you may want to be assertive and risk being fired or grounded. Consider the risk.

Procedure

- Leaders should demonstrate first.
- Divide the participants into groups of three.
- Start with the following *commercial* situation: saying "no" to a door-to-door salesperson who is selling raffle tickets for a charity.

- Instruct the participants to play their roles as follows:
  » *Asserter:* Responds *only* with, "I understand, but I'm not interested."
  » *Manipulator* (sales person): Makes statements such as: "What kind of person would do this?" "No one else has turned me down." "What would happen if everyone was like you?" "If you really cared about . . . ?" "Why don't you want it?"
  » *Coach* (helper): Comments on body language; keeps the asserter to the point; helps manipulator with statements if necessary.
- Have participants change groups and pick two persons with whom they have not worked.
- Ask them to role play a *peer* situation, such as when a friend wants to borrow something or go somewhere. Other requests from peers could be collecting for the school band, joining a club, or a friend asking with help babysitting a pet.
- Suggest an *authority* situation, parents or work. "Perhaps your supervisor has changed your work schedule for the good of the company, or your parents have grounded you for a week and you have made plans to go to a wonderful party." Suggest that the asserter respond with an accurate feeling, for example, to the supervisor, "I understand your problem but I'm not comfortable with that. Can we work something out?" To the parents, "I'm not trying to get out of my punishment, I deserve it, but is there something else we could work out so that I could go to the party?"
- Or try making excuses—when the *asserter* starts making excuses, the *manipulator* can argue about the excuse and draw the *asserter* away from her message.
- Discuss with the group their reactions to the exercise. What worked, what didn't. Ask for suggestions from the group to help with what didn't work.

Notes

🔖 Skill Instruction: Role Play Saying "No"

🕒 30 minutes

Purpose

- To support personal values.
- To use assertive skill of saying "no" in a personal situation.
- To build self esteem by experiencing taking control.

Materials

- Completed copies of previous exercise "I'm in Control" (A5-2)

Procedure

- In groups of four, each girl is going to take turns role playing the situation she worked through in the exercise "I'm in Control."
- Have each girl review her sheet and remind herself of her values and what and why she wants to do.
- One girl will be the asserter and tells her group just a few sentences that describes the situation.
- Two others will play her friends (peers) who will try to talk her into doing whatever it is she is feeling uncomfortable about.
- The fourth girl is the coach. Her job is to keep the asserter on track, remind her of the broken-record technique, her body language, and also to help the peer try manipulative measures.
- After each girl finishes her conversation to her satisfaction, the other three tell her what they liked about her behavior and then can give her suggestions about what they think can be improved. Was she assertive, passive, aggressive, passive-aggressive? When she was refusing, did any of you feel insulted, angry or hurt? How did you feel?
- The leaders circulate among the groups to keep things on track. Try to curtail long discursive explanations of the situation. Tell the group that you will be circulating and will listen in and be available for help.

Notes

Skill Instruction: Combining Persistence with Understanding and a Workable Compromise

⏲ 30 minutes

Purpose
- To show how persistence can be used to respond to legitimate points raised by the other person.
- To know when to allow the inclusion of an explanation in the asserter's refusal.

Materials
- Resource Sheet A5-3, newsprint or chalkboard with the following printed on it

---

Combining Broken Record with Understanding

Step 1. Their position (understanding)

Step 2. Your position (explanation)

Step 3. Action (your message)

Discussion
- Discuss persistence and understanding as follows:
  » Peer and family situations are often harder to handle than commercial or work situations. Usually a combination of empathy or understanding is effective. Remember that you are dealing with another person who has rights, problems, and feelings. Try to recognize these in your responses, be understanding and try to work things out if the requests are reasonable.
  » The broken-record technique can sound uncaring and mechanical if used too often. It may be better, especially with friends and family (those dear to you), to communicate in your response that you have listened to them and that you understand their position.
  » Look at the chart on Resource Sheet A5-3. Start with a statement showing that you understand the other person's problems or feelings. Always try to respond to what the other person actually said by summarizing his or her statements (your listening technique).
  » Next explain your position and note the differences between your position or opinion and theirs. Lastly, say what you want done or what you are going to do. Example: "I realize you worry about me when you don't know where I am (1), but I can't always get to a phone immediately (2), I will call you as soon as I can so please stop reminding me over and over again (3)."

- *Workable compromise:* If the other person is equally persistent, an assertive response is for you to negotiate a workable compromise. A compromise is assertive and workable if you are sure that afterward you will feel good about yourself and what you have done. In other words, you have said what you want, the other person has said he or she wants something different. To break the deadlock, one or the other of you suggests an alternative that both of you can accept.
- The more alternatives that are suggested, the better chance you have of developing a compromise you can accept. Ask yourself, "How else can we solve this problem? What else can we do?" Ask the other person the same questions.
- Note that when the asserter starts making excuses, this gives the manipulator a chance to argue about the excuse and draw the assertive away from her message. Example:
  » You: "I really don't have time to go shopping with you, I have a term paper to write and I promised my mother to come home early."
  » Manipulator: It won't take long, I need help in deciding on this shirt I saw, I helped you last time. we'll just run into this one store and no others."

Procedure

- Divide the participants into groups of three and have them take turns acting as asserter, requester, and coach.
- The *asserter* may be helpful, but it is not her responsibility to solve the other person's problems. She should repeat over and over her basic message of refusal. Remember how a manipulator operates. Do not forget to be understanding. Try a workable compromise if the request is important or if you wish to practice doing so.
- The *coach* may help the asserter keep to the basic message and/or help the requester manipulate.
- The asserter may refuse a request such as borrowing a car, collecting for the school band, hanging out, or joining a club, a friend asking for help babysitting a pet, or chose a situation of her own.
- Suggest that the asserter respond with "I understand your problem, but I feel anxious about lending my car," or disclose accurate feeling. Or "It sounds like fun, but I've decided to stay home tonight."
- The asserter may be helpful, but it is not their responsibility to solve the other person's problems. *Repeat over and over the basic message of refusal. Remember how a manipulator works.*
- Leaders should demonstrate using empathy and workable compromise before triads practice. Workable compromise: "I understand your problem, but I feel anxious about lending my car. I could drive you there."
- Try other situations:
  » Commercial – with clerks, servers
  » Mother-daughter relationships
  » Boyfriend-girlfriend relationships

» Situations involving friends or other relatives
» Pick a situation from their own experience

Discussion

- Ask the group for reactions to the role plays. What worked, what didn't. Ask for suggestions from the group to help with what didn't work.
- For more practice with the workable compromise see the supplemental exercise on negotiating (A5-7).

◆ Closing the Session

Purpose
- To provide closure for the group.
- Before closing the session, review and discuss the homework assignments.

Materials
- Close the session with The Link (A1-6).

Homework

📖 Readings
- True Stories 4 (A5-4)
- Helpful Hints for Saying "No" to Unfair Requests and Demands (A5-5)

◎ Activities
- Record in your journal your reactions to the following activities: refusing unreasonable requests; becoming aware of how you handle criticism; how you handled compliments you received; give two compliments and record how you gave them and how they were received; what is your "true-self" stone looking like now.
- Write a short paragraph or two describing your "true self." Bring to the next session to share if you wish.
- Supplemental Exercise: Negotiating or Reaching a Workable Compromise (A5-6)
- Supplemental Exercise: Keeping the Peace (A5-7)

Notes

❧ Supplemental Instruction: Negotiating or a Workable Compromise

🕐 15 minutes

Purpose
- To develop skills in negotiation.
- To practice talking about more intimate matters.
- To combine the skills of listening, making opinions known, persistence with values, feelings.

Materials
- Resource sheet (A5-6), extra copies of the observer's check list from Session 3 (A3-5)

Instructions
- Below is a scenario that also appears on Resource Sheet A5-6. Other scenarios can be suggested by group members.
- The situation involves a sexual situation. Leaders may choose whether or not to do this depending on the maturity of their group.
- The role playing can be done with two persons in front of the group playing A or B, or by having the participants break into groups of three. The third person will be the helper-observer.
- The helper-observer should use the observer's check list (A3-5).
- The scenario can be replayed with different people taking the roles or if one of the players is having a difficult time playing a role, someone else can jump in and take over.
- Discussion should follow the role-plays.

Scenario

A and B have been fooling around together at a party. Both have been drinking rather heavily. They have been slow dancing and making out on the dance floor.

Role A: Wants to leave the party and go out to someone's car where they can have more privacy.

Role B: Likes the attention of A and doesn't want to lose it, but is absolutely uneasy with being alone with A in the back seat of someone's car.

Directions

- Using the above as a scenario, negotiate a solution using some of the skills you learned—listening, expressing opinions, rights, and values, and working things out. One person can play A, another play B, and if you are in groups of three, a third can be the coach/observer. How can you work things out if you were B?
- If you wish, you may try a scenario of your own of a situation you know about.
- The helper-coach, using the check list passed out before, gives feedback on the assertive behavior and can jump in with suggestions if A or B gets stuck.

Session 6
Mistakes, Criticism, Feelings, and Needs

Overview

Goals
To teach the skills of admitting mistakes, handling criticism, and expressing feelings and needs assertively to show how these skills improve relationships and increase self-esteem.

Materials
Resource Sheets A6-1 through A6-10, newsprint or chalkboard, The Link (A1-6), marking pens, diary.

Teacher Instructions
Homework Review
Skill Instruction: Admitting Mistakes
Skill Instruction: Handling Criticism (Put-downs)
Skill Instruction: Expressing Feelings and Needs Assertively ("I" Language Assertion)
Skill Instruction: Keeping Cool to Critics (Fogging)
Closing the Session

Student Resource Sheets
Activity Sheet: Admitting Mistakes (A6-1)
Activity Sheet: Expressing Feelings and Needs Assertively (A6-2)
Activity Sheet: Keeping Your Cool (Fogging) (A6-3)
Helpful Hints for Dealing with Criticism or Anger (A6-4)
Helpful Hints for Expressing Dissatisfaction (A6-5)
Helpful Hints for Disagreeing (A6-6)
Activity Sheet: What Would You Say? (A6-7)
True Story 5 – Do You Act or React? (A6-8)
Supplemental Activity: Feeling Good Ideas (A6-9)
Supplemental Activity: Giving Criticism "Sandwiching" (A6-10)

Homework
Read Helpful Hints for Dealing with Criticism or Anger
Read Helpful Hints for Expressing Dissatisfaction
Read Helpful Hints for Disagreeing
True Story 5 – Do You Act or React?

❧ Homework Review

🕐 15 minutes

Purpose
- To evaluate understanding of concepts and movement toward improved self-esteem.
- To provide support for being able to refuse requests assertively and appropriately.

Materials
- Current journals, Resource Sheets A6-1 through A6-10, my true-self stone

Procedure
- Check journals.
- What do their "true-self" rocks look like this week?
- Ask them to display their rocks or objects so that everyone can admire them.
- Ask who would like to share their own true-self stories. Respond positively to each one.
- Ask for a volunteer to relate her experience in refusing a request. Give support and suggestions if necessary.

Notes

⊶ Skill Instruction: Admitting Mistakes

🕐 20 minutes

Purpose

- To introduce and allow practice in admitting mistakes.
- To increase self-esteem in learning an assertive skill that can diffuse criticism and gain respect.
- To improve interpersonal relationships.

Materials

- Resource Sheet A6-1

Discussion

- Discuss admitting mistakes as follows:
    » When you have made a mistake, the assertive way to handle it is to admit it. Not only do you defuse the criticism, but you also gain respect from others by showing that you are honest and responsible.
- You have a right to make mistakes. Everyone makes them. It's how we learn. A modern jet is off target over 90 percent of the time it is in flight. It is constantly correcting itself and realigning itself to its goal. If we can allow ourselves to make mistakes and know that the mistake has nothing to do with our basic goodness, we become happier and more successful and less fearful in life. No one is perfect.
- You take responsibility not only by admitting it, saying you are sorry, but also recognizing what the other person is feeling because of your mistake.
- Show empathy. Empathy means putting yourself in the other person's shoes. How would I feel if this happened to me?
- So the form of your apology goes something like this (leaders demonstrate): "You're right, I'm sorry. I made a mistake. You must be feeling very (irritated, upset, angry) about it. How can I make up for it?" The conversation can then go on to a more constructive discussion about how to correct the mistake.
- You can give one simple explanation for your mistake if you like, but if you go on and on about it, you will sound like you want the other person to feel sorry for you, that it's not your fault, and there is no reason for them to feel the way they do. A dead end will result with bad feelings on both sides—your guilt, their anger—(leaders demonstrate): "I'm really sorry, I'm late. This isn't my day, everything went wrong. I woke up feeling lousy, the shirt I wanted to wear was dirty, then I couldn't find my purse, my mother was arguing with me, and my watch was slow."

Procedure

- Divide the participants into pairs. Have each person take a turn practicing one of the following situations or use another experience of the participants choosing.

- » You have made a date to meet your best friend at the mall and arrive 20 minutes late.
- » You have borrowed a book from your teacher and lost it.
- » You borrowed the family car and got in an accident.
- » You are pregnant and must tell your parents.
- » You hurt a friend's feelings by saying something about them that you didn't know was a secret.
- » Talk about an experience of your own.
- Have the pairs continue the interchange until each person is satisfied with the results.
- Allow sufficient time after the exercise for the group members to share and discuss their reactions to the exercise as well as the implications for future behavior.

☙ Skill Instruction: Handling Criticism (Put-downs)

🕒 20 minutes

Purpose

- To teach participants how to handle criticism in a constructive manner without defensiveness
- To improve relationships
- To resolve interpersonal problems

Discussion

- Discuss handling criticism as follows:
    - » When someone criticizes you, remain calm, take a deep breath, and listen without interrupting. If the criticism is vague and general, you must help the criticizer become more specific so that you can see if the criticism has some truth to it or is a wrong perception that you can correct.
- If the criticism has some truth, you can then decide to keep or change the behavior.
- Here is an example that shows you how to get to the specifics. Leaders demonstrate:
    - » Criticism: "I don't like your attitude."
    - » Correct Response: "I don't understand. What is it about my attitude that you don't like?
    - » Criticism: "Well, you're too aggressive!"
    - » Response: "What was it about what I said or did that you think was aggressive?"
    - » Criticizer: "You always contradict me." (We're getting somewhere.)
    - » Response: "What is there about the contradiction that upsets you?"
    - » Criticizer: "You just don't seem to care about me anymore." (Aha, so that's it!)
    - » Response: "What do I do that makes you think I don't care anymore?"
    - » Criticizer: "You never seem to want to see the same movie I like or listen to my music or care about my opinions."
- Now you can talk about your specific behavior and whether it's true or not. Finish with "Is there anything else I should know?"
- Avoid using "why" questions as this arouses defensiveness. Instead, try to ask "what" or "how" after first saying, "I don't understand. How am I aggressive?" The phrase "I don't understand, what ___" is a good way to start.
- Ask the group, "How would you respond to the statement: "You never do anything right?" Response from group: "I don't understand. What don't I do right?"

Procedure

- Divide the participants into groups of three. Have them take turns role playing a following situation:
    - » Friend says to friend, "You make me so mad!"

- » Parent to daughter, "You don't appreciate all I've done for you."
- » You to school friend: "What do you think of my report?" Your friend has trouble criticizing but you really need some help before you turn it in. You can help her by saying something like "I'm not satisfied with this section, can you suggest something?" and then "What about the next section?" "Is there anything else?"

- In each role play, one person acts as the criticizer, one as the responder (the asserter), and one as the coach.
- The coach helps the asserter with phrasing and deciding when the situation is specific enough to begin to resolve the issue. The coach also should give feedback on assertive verbal and nonverbal behavior. Listen to humor, it may be a disguise for more put-downs and teasing.

☙ Skill Instruction: Expressing Feelings and Needs Assertively ("I" Language)

🕐 20 minutes

Purpose

- To learn a nondefensive way to express feelings and needs.
- To improve personal relationships
- To improve self-esteem

Materials

- Resource Sheet A6-2, list the four steps of "I" language assertion on newsprint or chalkboard

---

☑ Step 1. "I . . . "
☑ Step 2. "When . . . "
☑ Step 3. "I feel . . . "
☑ Step 4. "I'd like . . . "

Discussion

- Discuss "I" language assertion as follows:
  » Assertion training emphasizes not blaming or ridiculing the other person. When you start your conversation with the word "you" as in "You did this," or "You made me," the other person feels attacked and their first impulse is to fight back rather than listen to you. Before you know it you are in an argument rather than working out a problem.
- Helpful criticism focuses on specific behavior rather than what the person is or is not.
- The four step model is especially effective in expressing feelings, both positive and negative, in asserting rights and needs or asking for favors.
- Let's look at Resource Sheet A6-2:
  » Step 1. "I . . . " This is where you describe how the other person's behavior affects your behavior or feelings. If your behavior is not affected, you may be dealing with a difference in values. You still have the right to express your feelings, but will need to consider the other person's rights or values.
  » Step 2. "When . . . " You describe as factually as possible the specific behavior that either pleases or troubles you.
  » Step 3. "I feel . . . " You describe your present feelings. Leave this part out if it's not appropriate as in some commercial situations.

» Step 4. "I'd like . . . "You describe what you want to do about the problem if it is appropriate to the situation.

- With "I" language assertion you take the responsibility for your own feelings instead of blaming the other person (I get angry versus you make me angry). Example: I don't like it (Step 1) when I'm made fun of in front of other people (Step 2). I feel embarrassed and get really angry (Step 3). When you have some kind of problem with me, I'd like you to talk to me about it when we are alone (Step 4).

- You might like to change the step order to suit your own speech pattern. **Example:** When you leave me alone at a party where I don't know anybody (Step 2), I feel rejected and embarrassed (Step 3), and want to hide in a corner (Step 1). I would like you to stay with me for awhile and introduce me to some of the others first (Step 4).

- You do not always use all four steps. "I" feel may not be appropriate in commercial situations. **Example:** "I can't eat this fish (Step 1), it tastes spoiled (Step 2), I would like to order something else (Step 4). If you are criticizing a commercial service, complain privately to the person responsible soon after you notice the problem. Don't apologize. Be specific and try to compliment the person first, "Your food is usually wonderful and I enjoy coming here but I . . . " Criticize only those actions where change is possible.

- To summarize, when you use "I" language assertion you:
  » Talk about the person's specific behavior instead of attacking him or her.
  » Avoid using the word "you" as much as possible.
  » Talk about the way the behavior troubles you.
  » Take responsibility for your own feelings instead of blaming them on the other person.
  » Suggest the specific behavior you would like the other person to change or suggest how the two of you might solve the problem.

Procedure

- Now we will try different ways of expressing ourselves first so that we can actually see how using "you" instead of "I" affects us.
- Have the participants divide into pairs and take turns dealing with one of the situations listed below. First start with the word "you" then start with an "I" statement. For example when your sister leaves her clothes all over your room. The leader demonstrates by looking angrily at one of the participants and says, "You're so messy! This place is a pig pen!" The leader asks the person how she felt being spoken to that way. Then the leader uses "I" statements to the same person: "When you leave your clothes all over the room, (Step 1) I can't even find a place to sit down (Step 2). I feel my space has been invaded (Step 3). Can we work something out?"(Step 4)
- Situations:
  » Ask someone to quiet down so you can study, he's playing loud music.
  » Tell someone he or she did not do his or her share.
  » A friend of yours has blabbed your secret to someone at school.

- » Your date has taken you to an expensive restaurant and show and now thinks he is entitled to have sex in return.
- » Your boyfriend wont stop pressuring you to use drugs or loses his temper a lot and you want to break up.
- » You're at a slumber party and the girls are deciding to play a mean and hurtful trick on another girl. You don't think it's right.

- Ask for feedback from the group about how the "I" statements worked:
  - » How they felt when the asserter started with "you"?
  - » How was it with "I"?

⊷ Skill Instruction: Keeping Cool to Critics (Diversion)

🕒 15 minutes

Purpose

- To desensitize participants to *destructive* criticism.
- To help with self-control.

Materials

Resource Sheet A6-3, display these four phrases somewhere in the room

> **"You're right, I'm sorry."**
> **"Yes, that's probably true."**
> **"That could be true."**
> **"I can see how you think that."**

Discussion

- Leaders discuss as follows:
  » Criticism is really hard for most of us. When you're tied up in knots, feeling attacked, there's no way you can focus on the matter at hand, much less be assertive.
  » Diversion is *not* assertive and has only limited value. It is like protective armor you use while you decide how to respond. It is also a technique to use with people who will not listen, who argue for the sake of arguing, or with whom you have tried to be assertive and failed.
  » Diversion protects you from people who think their values are better than yours, those who are not interested in hearing your side and only want to wear you down. *It is useful only as a last resort—to shut off further argument.*
- How to respond:
  » Now, practically every statement of criticism has some truth to it. Your response is to agree to whatever part is true. For example, "You made a mistake!" or "You got tomato sauce all over my blouse!" you respond with "You're right, I'm sorry."
  » If it is true in principle or reasoning, e.g., "If you stay out late every night, you'll get sick," you respond with, "That could be true."
  » If the odds are that it might be true, e.g., "Anybody who believes that must be simple minded," you respond with, "That could be true."
  » If you can't agree to any part of the criticism, you respond with, "I can see how you might think that."

Procedure

- The leaders may want to model the exercise first, with the group hurling criticisms at them.
- Divide the participants into new groups of three. Have them act out the following roles:
  » *Diverter:* responds to all criticism with any of the above statements and only the above.
  » *Attacker:* criticizes everything about the diverter's appearance—clothing, posture, facial expression, hair style, manner of speaking, etc.
  » *Coach:* helps the diverter respond with one of the four responses, then, as the attacker runs out of criticism, switches to helping the attacker think of barbs.
- Bring the exercise to a close by saying to the group: "You're not very good at this, are you?" "You need more practice, don't you?" "In fact, you're so terrible, you need lots more practice." Point to the chart as a hint for how they should reply.

Closing the Session

Purpose
- Before closing the session, discuss the homework assignment with the participants.

Materials
- Close the session with The Link (A1-6) exercise

Homework
    📖 Readings
- Helpful Hints for Dealing with Criticism or Anger (A6-4)
- Helpful Hints for Expressing Dissatisfaction (A6-5)
- Helpful Hints for Disagreeing (A6-6)
- True Story 5 – Do You Act or React? (A6-8)

    ◎ Activities
- What Would You Say? (A-6-7)
- Start a joke collection. Bring one to the next session. Lighten up and laugh a little. Using humor can ease tense or embarrassing situations. It can get your message across in a nonthreatening way and can improve relationships. Why should guys be the only ones to tell jokes?
- Record in your journal: any attempts at assertive behavior; reactions to helping someone (carry groceries, cut the grass, shovel snow, walk a dog, babysit)
- Keep track of your "true-self" rock

Notes

Session 7
Social Skills

Overview

☼ **Goals**
- To learn social skills to gain more confidence. Integrate the skills and learning concepts of the workshop and provide carry-over to real- life situations.

✎ **Materials** Resource Sheets A7-1 through A7-9, newsprint, markers, diary.

Teacher Instructions
Homework Review
Skill Exercise: Conversations or the Game of Catch
Skill Instruction: Breaking Into Conversations
Skill Instruction: Behavior Rehearsal with Muscle
Aftereffects – Setting Goals
Post-Session Self-Assessment
Closing the Session and Ending the Workshop
Skill Exercise: You're Awesome!

Student Resource Sheets
Activity: Starting Conversations or the Game of Catch (A7-1)
Ending Conversations (A7-2)
Activity: Behavior Rehearsal with Muscle (A7-3)
Activity: Aftereffects – Setting Goals (A7-4)
Post-Session Self-Assessment (A7-5)
Activity: Step by Step to Responsible Assertion (A7-6)
What Life Is All About (A7-7)
Feeling Good Two (A7-8)
Supplemental Activity: Setting Goals – Aftereffects Two (A7-9)

Homework
Read What Life Is All About (A7-7)
Reminder: Step by Step to Responsible Assertion (A7-6)
Activity: Feeling Good Two (A7-8)
Supplemental Activity: Setting Goals – After Effects Two (A7-9)

✥ Homework Review

⏲ 20 minutes

Purpose
- To reinforce assertive behavior.
- To start the transition into application for real-life situations.
- To lay the groundwork for improving social skills.

Materials
- Resource Sheet A6-7

Discussion
- Ask for experiences in helping other people. How did they feeling helping someone? What was the reaction of the people they helped? Tell them. "Helping others is a good way to help yourself too—to get yourself out of a funk."
- Explain why they were asked to collect jokes:
  » A good sense of humor is a great social skill. If you are able to see the funny side of things, you can relieve a tense situation, you can rescue someone or yourself from an embarrassing moment. Showing a sense of humor is a big step toward getting along with many people.
  » *The shortest distance between two people is a good laugh.* —Victor Borge
  » Selena was having dinner in a very expensive restaurant as a guest of her boyfriend's parents. There were many courses, each with its own set of forks and spoons. By the time the waiter came to clear the table for dessert, she noticed that everyone had used all the utensils that had been set out. Selena still had one lonely fork left. She was sure everyone noticed it too. As the waiter was resetting the table, giving everyone except Selena new forks, she remarked, "I brought that one from home." Everyone laughed and proceeded with their dessert.
- Leader asks each one to share their joke with the group.
- Check their journals for experiences with assertive behavior.
- What does their "true-self" rock look like this week?
- Have the group divide into two's and go over their What Would You Say activity sheets together (A6-7).
- Have them come together in a circle and each one pick one of the statements to tell the group. Ask the group to react. Ask if anyone had a different way of making the assertive statement, showing that there are different ways to be assertive. There are no right or wrong answers.

Skill Exercise: Starting Conversations or the Game of Catch

⏰ 30 minutes

Purpose

- To increase self-esteem by learning an important social skill.
- To learn the difference between excellent and poor conversational skills.

Materials

- Resource Sheets A7-1 and A7-2, newsprint or chalkboard.

Discussion

- The leaders start the exercises on conversations by reminding the group that they have already had some practice on other social skills: introducing themselves, giving and receiving compliments, listening, handling put-downs, admitting mistakes. This one is comparatively easy—how to carry on a conversation.

- Conversations are like a game of catch. Someone starts by throwing out the ball, the other person catches it and throws it back. You can start a conversation anywhere, waiting in line, in the dentist's waiting room, at a party. Where else? List the suggestions on newsprint or chalkboard.

- Contrary to what you may think, people usually meet you halfway in beginning a conversation. The best time is when the person looks approachable, when he or she is not busy and is smiling. However, you can also start by saying " Excuse me, do you know where I can find . . . " Or some other question.

- You learned how to introduce yourself at the beginning of this workshop. Let's do some review. You begin with a simple, "Hi, my name is _____," then pause and let that person introduce him or herself. Then listen. If you don't catch the name and a lot of people don't because they are thinking of what they will say next, ask the person to spell it. Names are important to people and they are flattered that you care enough to get it right.

- After the introduction, you toss out the ball again by asking a question or making a comment about your surroundings or what's happening right then. "I wonder why this line is so long," or "What do you think of the band," or "How do you know the hostess?"

- To keep the conversation going avoid questions that can be answered by a simple "yes" or "no" or with a single word. And do your part by tossing the ball back with a new question or statement.

- These are dropping-the-ball conversation stoppers: "Do you like this band?" "Yes." "I heard that new math teacher is really hard." "Oh, really." "Is there a Coke machine around here?" "I don't know."

- These are accepting the ball and tossing it back. "The band's okay, I like their selections but I think the bass isn't very good. What do you think?" "Oh, really? Where did you hear that the math teacher is hard?" "I don't know where the Coke machine is. I haven't seen one. Let's look farther down the hall."

- Of course you show you are interested by your body language. Keep your eyes on the person, lean forward, and smile.
- If you start a conversation and you don't get good listening cues, it doesn't necessarily mean she or he doesn't want to talk, maybe he or she is unskilled in making conversation.

Procedure

- Turn to Resource Sheet A7-1 and pick two situations, write what you would say in these situations and then we will practice.
- Next, we will practice how to end the conversation. Look at the directions on Resource Sheet A7-2.

Skill Instruction: Breaking into Conversations

⏱ 15 minutes

Purpose
- To explore effective ways to break into conversations in social occasions.
- To gain confidence by practicing a social skill.

Materials
- Chalkboard or newsprint, markers

Procedure
- Divide the participants into groups of four or five and ask for a volunteer who has trouble breaking into conversations or select a someone.
- Ask the other group members to stand close together and start a conversation on any topic—the weather, a vacation, a movie, a book, or shopping.
- Have the newcomer try to join the group and enter the conversation.
- Suggest that the participants watch for the following:
    » Length of time before the newcomer spoke.
    » Did the newcomer add to the conversation or bring things to a halt?
    » Where did the newcomer position herself?
    » Was her statement a new topic?
    » How did the others respond to it?
- After a few minutes of conversation, ask the group members to give feedback to the newcomer on what was both effective and not aggressive. What worked best in her being included in the group with comfort for everybody.
- Call the groups together and ask them what would be the most helpful hints for joining a group conversation they discovered during this exercise.
- List them on the chalkboard or newsprint and ask them to record them in their journals.

Notes

✒ Skill Instruction: Behavior Rehearsal with Muscle

🕐 45 minutes

Purpose

- To provide practice using real-life situations of the participants choosing.
- To integrate several already practiced procedures.
- To facilitate the transition from structured exercises to complex behavior.

Materials

- Resource Sheet A7-3

Procedure

- Have each person think of a situation in which she has difficulty acting assertively and complete the activity sheet. It may be a situation that she is facing soon, something she has listed as being difficult in her presession self-assessment or a situation that she felt she didn't handle satisfactorily in the past.
- Leaders demonstrate the exercise as described below. One leader will be the asserter and describe the situation to three group members who line up in a row. Standing will better show body language.
- During the exercise leaders should go from group to group providing assistance as needed. Inform the groups that you will be doing this.

Exercise

- Move into small groups of four. Stand in a line. Each person in turn follows the steps below.
    » The first person *briefly* describes the situation to her group.
    » Then she acts as the asserter and makes her assertive statement to the second person in line. The second person does *not* respond. This first attempt is a try out of the words and body language.
    » Using the assertion check list, the group members give positive feedback, telling the asserter specifically what they thought was assertive about her body language and how she communicated.
    » The asserter is asked what she would like to improve and asks the others for one or two suggestions.
    » The asserter then incorporates the feedback in the original assertion to the third person in line.
    » Now, the third person responds with a mild argument. The asserter responds to the argument as assertively as possible.
    » The group gives feedback as above.
    » Incorporating the feedback the asserter makes the assertion again to the fourth person who responds with a much stronger argument.

- » The group gives feedback as described in the steps above.
- » Bring the groups back as a whole and ask for comments. What did they learn? Was it helpful?
* Most situations will be easier to handle than this. But this prepares them in case they are not.

☙ Aftereffects – Setting Goals

⏱ 15 minutes

Purpose
- To set goals for continuing progress.
- To apply skills in the real world.

Materials
- Resource Sheet A7-4

Discussion
- Well, we can't stop now, just when you've gotten started on the road to strength and higher self-esteem. This last activity will help you set some goals for yourself so that you can continue to apply what you've learned so far.

Procedure
- Turn to Resource Sheet A7-4 and complete the activity sheet.
- Go over instructions and make sure everyone understands them.
- Have one or two persons volunteer to share their goals and baby steps to check on understanding.
- Talk about possible rewards.
- Talk about who can be counted on for support.

❧ Post-Session Self-Assessment

◷ 5 minutes

Purpose
- To measure improvement compared to beginning of workshop.
- To see which areas still need work.

Materials
- Resource Sheet A7-5

Procedure
- Have participants complete post-session self-assessment.
- Ask for comments on any changes.

Closing the Session and Ending the Workshop

Purpose
- To bring closure to the group.
- To set post workshop goals and suggest effective steps to continue progress.
- To plan for other resources for support when the workshop is over.
- To celebrate achievements.

Materials
- Resource Sheets A7-6 to A7-7

Discussion
- Review and discuss the final homework assignments (A7-6 through A7-7)
  - Read Step by Step to Responsible Assertion
  - Read What Life Is All About
  - Activity: Feeling Good Two
- Discuss post-workshop strategies for the participants, including:
  - Giving themselves rewards for each step toward reaching their goals
  - Using resources for additional support when the workshop is over
    - Other members of the group
    - Friends
    - Family
- Have the group suggest activities that they could do at home that would make them feel good, such as:
  - A giggle bulletin board with photos of themselves and friends in wild crazy poses or the best of the worst, cartoons, jokes, baby pictures, fun messages, and invitations.
  - Create a peaceful place with a favorite picture, plant, objects.
  - Before going to sleep, think of some of the things they feel good about doing that day such as, talked to my sister, hung up my clothes, took a long walk, did my homework, bought a flower for friend.
  - Start a gratitude journal keeping track of the positive things that happen to them.
- End the session with the Skill Exercise: You're Awesome! on the following page.

Notes

✌ Skill Exercise: You're Awesome!

🕐 15 minutes

Purpose
- To provide closure to the workshop.
- To allow participants to leave with a positive experience.

Discussion
- Appreciative words are the most powerful force for good on earth. Ask "How do you feel when some tells you something nice about yourself?"
- Everyone wants to be acknowledged and appreciated. When you tell someone how much you appreciate them, it makes them feel really good about themselves and you and they are more likely to pass the appreciation on to others which makes everyone feel better.
- Tell the group something like, "We've spent a lot of time together the past few weeks and have learned to know each other pretty well and learned a lot from each other. Let's tell one another how much we appreciate them and what we like about them."

Procedure
- Have participants stand or sit in a semi-circle.
- Each girl takes a turn standing in front of the group.
- Members of the group take turns and tell this person a sincere appreciation. Examples: "I love your playfulness," "You've been so helpful," You are kind," "You are special," "You are strong."
- Another version would be to give each other neat nicknames; "Golden One," "Sunshine," "Sunflower," "Star."
- Leaders need to be prepared to fill any gaps. Don't allow time for any painful and embarrassing silences.
- End with a group hug.

Appendix A
Resource Sheets

Resource Sheet A1-1

Presession Self-Assessment

Identify how comfortable you feel in each of the areas listed on the following page. If there are other areas of assertion you would like to work on, write them in the blanks at the bottom of the grid.

Most girls have trouble being assertive with certain types of people, for example, you may feel comfortable asking for a favor from your parents but not from boy friends. If this is so, in each column put (b) for boys, (g) for girls, (p) for parents, or (t) for teachers. Since this sheet will only be seen by you, just fill it out so that you will understand which areas you would like to improve.

At the end of the workshop you will fill out a form like this again and compare the two so that you can see how you improved.

Assertive Skill	Comfortable	Need More Practice	Uncomfortable
Saying "no"			
Asking for favors			
Making requests			
Expressing positive feelings			
Expressing negative feelings			
Giving compliments			
Receiving compliments			
Giving constructive criticism			
Receiving constructive criticism			
Expressing opinions			
Meeting new people			
Starting conversations			
Continuing conversations			
Talking about yourself			
Admitting mistakes			
Apologizing when at fault			
Handling other people's anger			
Expressing needs			
Asking for information from clerks			
Asking for information from teachers			
Asking for help			
Asking for explanations			

Resource Sheet A1-2

Getting from Here to There

The workshop will have four training steps:
- Learning to tell assertive behavior from aggressive and nonassertive behaviors
- Identifying personal rights and accepting them as well as respecting the rights of others
- Reducing blocks to acting assertively
- Developing skills through role playing and practice

Expectations for participants:
- Based on attendance and participation in all seven sessions of the workshop, it is expected you will:
  » decide which are the situations in which you would like to be able to express what you feel assertively
  » be able to distinguish assertive behavior from aggressive and nonassertive behavior
  » examine and clarify your beliefs about your rights and those of the people with whom you are communicating
  » understand how those rights are related to assertive behavior
  » learn how certain feelings make it difficult to be assertive but easy to be aggressive or nonassertive
  » have several opportunities to practice standing up for your opinions and needs without violating the rights of others
  » feel stronger, respected, and more in control of your life
  » be free to refuse to participate in any activity; no reasons need to be given as long as you do so in a manner that does not interfere with the choices and participation of other members
  » keep a daily journal of the results of your practice behavior (homework) outside of the workshop and record in your journal feelings, thoughts, ideas, and opinions
  » keep confidential any information shared during discussions of the group

Expectations for workshop leader(s):
- It is expected that the leader(s) will:
  » use education and training skills to teach assertive behavior
  » provide within the session for the practice of assertive skills
  » teach skills to reduce blocks to assertive behavior
  » be prepared, model assertive behavior, and be present every week
  » respect the right of any participant to refuse to participate in any activity as long as it doesn't interfere with the participation of the other members
  » keep confidential any information discussed during in the group

Methods and procedures:

- We will meet for about two hours weekly for seven weeks during which our sessions will include:
    - » discussions, demonstrations, questionnaires, paper-and-pencil exercises, short homework assignments, and behavior rehearsals or role-playing
    - » focus on behaviors such as dealing with criticism and "put-downs," persistence, asking for help or favors, saying "no" to unreasonable requests, resisting what makes us uncomfortable or guilty, making reasonable compromises, and expressing opinions

Resource Sheet A1-3

Keeping Confidences

Scenario

Megan is off stage. Brittany is in the group.

The first person, Karla, tells the group, "I dropped my books in the hall yesterday and this real cool guy picked them up for me. He was so cute and so nice! His name is Josh and he sits two rows ahead of me in home room. I have been seeing Brian but now I think I like Josh better. I'm thinking about dropping Brian. But I don't know how to tell him."

Karla leaves.

The next day, Brittany, a member of the group, meets Megan.

Megan: Hey, how's the group going?

Brittany: Just great. Yesterday my friend, Karla wanted to know how to dump Brian because she just met this great guy Josh.

Megan: Really. Hmmm, that's interesting.

Brittany leaves. Karla arrives.

Megan meets Karla and says: "Hey, I just heard you were going to dump Brian. Mind if I ask him to the movies?"

Megan leaves. Brittany arrives. Karla meets Brittany.

Karla to Brittany: You weren't supposed to tell anyone about what's said in the group. How come you did that? I thought you were my friend."

Resource Sheet A1-4

What Is Assertive Behavior?

Assertive behavior means standing up for yourself without hurting others. You can say what you think, feel, and believe in a direct, confident, honest, and polite way without hurting others.

Aggressive behavior goes to the extreme. People who are aggressive must get their way without regard for the feelings or rights of other people. They stand up for themselves all right but they want to win or dominate and end up making the other person feel insulted, humiliated, angry, and confused.

Nonassertive or passive people let others make decisions for them. They don't say what they want, sometimes don't know what they want, or speak in such an apologetic, cautious, non-confident manner that they are ignored.

Passive-aggressive behavior means not standing up for yourself at first and then sabotaging the situation later so that the other person feels guilty, punished, or angry.

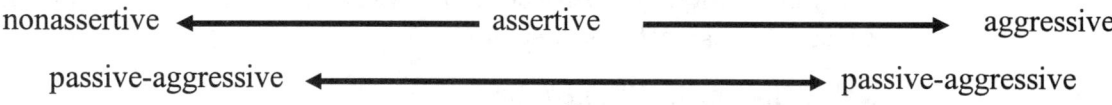

Assertive behavior is half way between the two extremes.

How Can I Tell When I Am Assertive?

- When you:
    » stand up for your rights and let other people do the same
    » can say no when you do not want to say yes to someone's request
    » can express positive feelings to other people and what they do
    » can express negative feelings to others about what they do without being abusive or cruel
    » can receive compliments without denying them
    » can take criticism without excuses
    » can start and carry on conversations
    » can recognize and express your good points
    » can ask for what is rightfully yours
    » feel good about yourself and in control of yourself after experiencing any of the above

Does Being Assertive Mean You "Win" or Get Your Way All the Time?

- No. Often it means you compromise, but do not feel you have "lost."
- Often it means it means you increase your chances to work things out to your satisfaction at a later time even if you are not completely satisfied now.

📄 **Resource Sheet A1-5**

Your Comfort Level

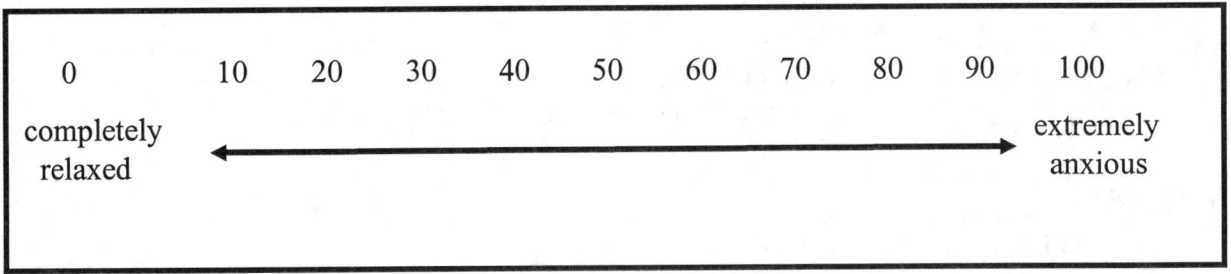

Homework

Readings

- Getting from Here to There (A1-2)
- Keeping Confidences (A1-3)
- What Is Assertive Behavior (A1-4)
- How Keeping a Journal Helps and True Story 1 – Lisa's Story (A1-7)

Activities

- Do Discrimination Quiz (A1-8)
- Record in your journal: introduce yourself to three strangers. How did you feel before, during, and after the behavior?
- Observe three situations. Record in your journal how you or others behaved as illustrated in the example provided in Appendix F. At this point, you are learning to identify the different kinds of behavior—not practice them.
- Write down three things you accomplished each day (A1-9). Did you clean your room, make your bed, do your homework? Remember the small accomplishments.

Resource Sheet A1-6

The Link

- Today I learned that . . .
- I wish that . . .
- Right now I feel . . .
- I was pleased . . .
- This session helped me to . . .
- I will think more about . . .
- What I like about myself is . . .
- Next time I'd like to . . .

Resource Sheet A1-7

How Keeping a Diary Helps

A diary is any book, spiral notebook, or blank pages you use to jot down your feelings, happenings, goals, ideas, observations about your behavior or reactions to events around you. Writing in a diary helps you to tune in to your thoughts and feelings and better understand yourself. By seeing your words on paper, you can be more objective. You can stand back and view yourself. This will help you to clarify your feelings and ideas so that when the next chance comes along to voice them you will be more sure of yourself and what you believe.

You don't have to write a lot or even every day. As we go through this workshop and you try different behaviors you will become more aware of your feelings and thoughts and more aware of how people respond to you. What does it mean? Think of the diary as a place where you can express yourself and your ideas about what is taking place. Sometimes, if you wish you may want to share what you wrote. But diaries are private so it is up to you.

True Story 1 – Lisa's Story

It's pretty interesting to be working on a book with my mother, of all people. The most interesting thing about it is how easy and fun it is to work with her. I am amazed. I can remember, not really so long ago, when she was *the enemy*. She was always on my case about everything: I should comb my hair, stop wearing such sloppy clothes, shave my legs, clean my room, stand up straight, keep my elbows off the table, do the dishes, hang out with different friends. As far as she was concerned nothing I did or said was ever right or good enough. (Of course nothing she said or did was cool enough for me either. I didn't want to be caught dead with her. Those hair sprayed helmet hairdos and pant suits . . . give me a break!) Well, I sure showed her, I turned out pretty okay. And she sure showed me. She's more than okay. I couldn't ask for a more wonderful Mom.

The funny thing is that she now looks back on my teen years with nostalgia. I remember her crying every day.

When I think back on those years, I remember being pretty scared. There was so much pressure from all sides to be a certain way I thought I would explode. In fact I did. Mostly at my mother. Everybody else, I was desperately trying to get them to like me, or at least not reject me. Since at that time being rich and blond and beautiful was in (I think it still is), I started off with a handicap. I felt like the ugliest duck and unfortunately I believed looks were everything. There wasn't a lot I could do about that problem except pray, so I had to really get the other stuff right. I could not afford to be uncool. Being uncool was admitting you didn't know something, saying something dumb, not knowing something about sex, not getting a joke, liking the wrong music, looking stupid when you dance, wearing uncool stuff from K-Mart, and in my particular, sub-crowd, getting B's or less. I found out early on that it was pretty risky to say what you liked or didn't like. You could get it wrong. So I would wait to hear from the cooler kids what was okay to like.

The trouble with that was that I never learned to look inside to find out what I liked. Not only was it too dangerous (what if what I liked wasn't cool?) but what was inside me was such a tangled jumble of fears, insecurities, and funny conflicting feelings that I think if anyone had asked me to go inside myself and really feel what I felt, I probably would have put my hands over my ears and screamed. At the time I just thought I was really weird and sooner or later someone was going to find out and they definitely were not going to understand.

It wasn't until I grew up that I found out that everyone feels weird and everyone hopes to be understood.

I didn't even feel safe and at home in my own skin. My body was doing all kinds of things that felt like total betrayals. Breaking out. Oh God! As if I wasn't already geeky enough? Periods? What on earth is the point of that! And my body was changing and totally freaking me out. (Hips? Not hips! Breasts are okay but hips?). If only there was someplace I could go to feel safe. To feel secure. To feel love with no expectations. To feel good about myself.

I didn't find out that such a place existed until much later. (I also didn't find out that I was a cool, attractive babe until much later either.) But I get to tell you now that this place does exist and it is incredible. It is safe and beautiful and magical and free. And the best part about it is that it's portable. You don't need to ask anyone to drive you there. It goes with you everywhere. It's lightweight and unbreakable and always perfect. And your True Self, the part of you that is pure love and magic, lives there.

Where is this place? You've probably guessed. It is inside of each of you. We're going to show you the way to this incredible place, and once you've been there you can go back anytime you want. And it won't cost a dime of your allowance.

Does "expressing your views and feelings" mean you say whatever is on your mind? Do you just let your feelings out all the time, with everyone?
- No. For example, you may get temporary satisfaction if you tell your best friend to "go to hell," but the long-range effect could be losing her as a friend altogether.

Should I always be assertive?
- That is up to you. You are free to choose not to assert yourself.

How do I decide when to be assertive?
- Ask yourself three questions:
  » How important is this to me?
  » How will I feel afterward?
  » How much risk do I take? What will I have to give up? What are the consequences?
- Don't scare yourself with unlikely probabilities. Ask yourself, "How much chance is there of this happening?

Why do I need to be assertive?
- Because big changes happen to you as a teenager becoming an adult. Many young people feel scared and uncertain. Teens often face serious decisions about school, work,

friends, and even sex. Many teens face temptations like alcohol and drugs. Being assertive makes it easier for you to make the decision that fits you the best.

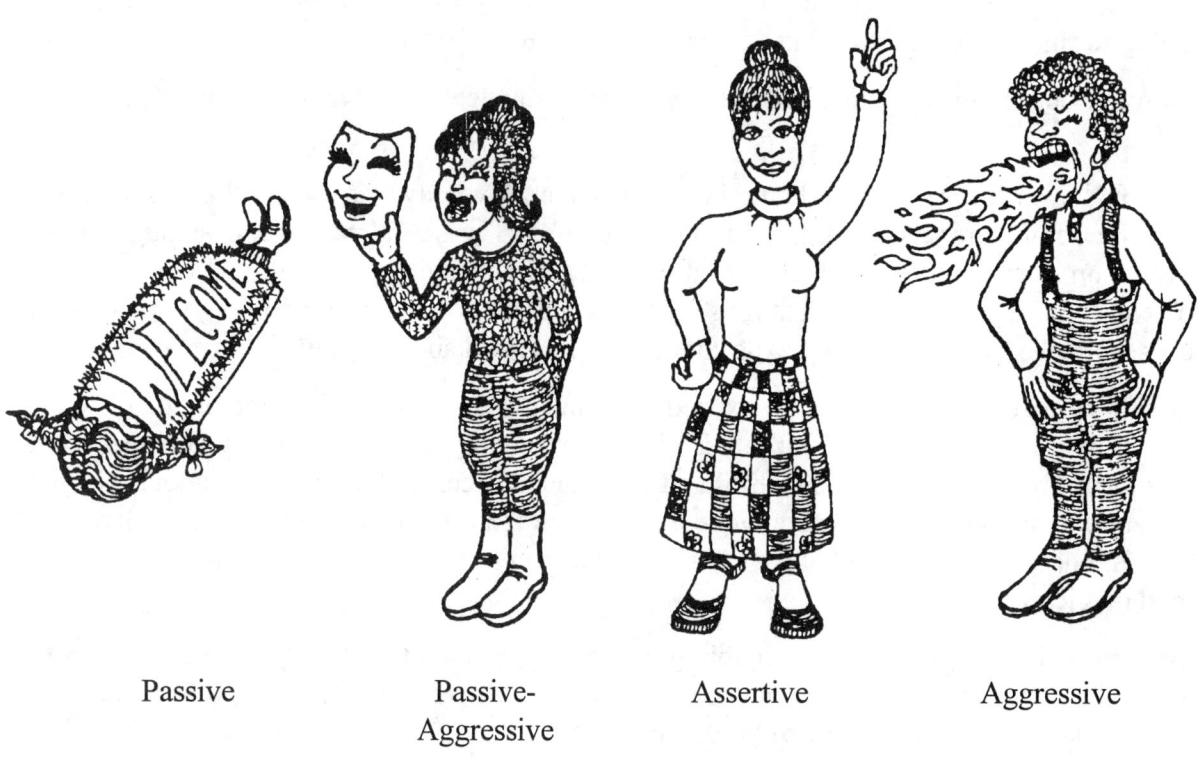

Passive   Passive-Aggressive   Assertive   Aggressive

📄 **Resource Sheet A1-8**

Homework Activity: Discrimination Quiz

N = Nonassertive AG = Aggressive
A = Assertive PAG = Passive Aggressive

Write either N, A, AG, or PAG after each response.

Situation	Response
A good friend calls and tells you she desperately needs you to help sell tickets to raise money for the band.	You do not want to do it, so you make up a story, "Oh gee, I just know my mom will be mad at me if I say yes. She says I'm already involved in too many things. She'll really get on my case if I take on another project." _____
You are at a school project meeting with seven guys. At the first meeting the chairman asks you to be the secretary.	"No! I'm sick and tired of being the secretary just because I'm the only girl in the group." _____
Your project has progressed, but you are doing all the planning, paper work, etc.	"Hey guys, this is supposed to be a team project but I see I'm doing all the work. I'd like to talk about sharing the work load. _____
A guy asks you for a date. You have dated him once before and you are not interested in dating him again.	You say, "I'm not sure about that day, let me call you back," and you never do. _____
The library calls and asks you to return a book that you never checked out.	You respond, "What are you talking about? You people better get your records straight. I never had that book and don't try to make me pay for it." _____
You are in line at the supermarket and are in a hurry. Someone behind you has one item and asks to get in front of you.	"I realize that you don't want to wait in line, but I was here first and I really need to get out of here." _____
Your sister always leaves your room a mess.	You say, "You're a mess and our room is always a mess and just because I'm the oldest, mom always blames me. It's not fair." _____
A boy in school is being obnoxious, making remarks about your looks, your clothes, bumping into you.	You say, "I want you to stop talking to me like that. I'm sure you don't realize how embarrassing it is, I'd rather you just say "Hi." _____
Your little brother has interrupted you three times with something unimportant. You already have asked him not to interrupt you.	"I can't listen to you and talk on the phone at the same time. I'll be on the phone a few more minutes and then we'll talk." _____
Some kids in your gang have started smoking cigarettes and want you to smoke with them.	You know it is bad for you, you can't stand the smell but you want to be cool. You try it, hate it, hide them from your parents, but keep on smoking. _____

Resource Sheet A1-9

Three Things I Did Today

Instructions: Make a list of three things you are proud you did each day. Some examples are making your bed, washing the dishes, walking the dog, feeding the cat, turning in your math paper, taking your little sister to the movies, doing well on a test, making a new friend.

First Day:
1.
2.
3.

Second Day:
1.
2.
3.

Third day:
1.
2.
3.

Fourth Day
1.
2.
3.

Fifth Day
1.
2.
3.

Sixth Day
1.
2.
3.

Seventh Day
1.
2.
3.

📄 **Resource Sheet A1-10**

Supplemental Activity:
Do I Have Trouble With Any of These?

Check "yes" or "no" next to each sentence below.

Yes	No	
❏	❏	I can't seem to think of what to say when I get a compliment.
❏	❏	I'm really flustered and upset when someone gets angry with me.
❏	❏	I can't seem to let people know that I disagree with them.
❏	❏	I let myself be talked into doing something wrong.
❏	❏	Even though I didn't like the food that was served to me, I ate it without saying anything.
❏	❏	I seem to apologize for things I don't do or aren't my fault.
❏	❏	I pick my clothes so that I will look like and be accepted by my friends.
❏	❏	I have trouble asking for help.
❏	❏	I can never think of what to say to start a conversation.
❏	❏	I can't seem to make myself heard when I'm with a group.

Bring this resource sheet to each session. At the end of the workshop go over this list again to see if you have trouble with fewer items.

Resource Sheet A2-1

True Story 2 – I Like Me

Tia reported in one session of an assertion training workshop that she had been playing tennis with a boy who reached over the net to hit the ball back to her. Finally she spoke up and said, "I believe it's against the rules to return the ball before it crosses the net."

I asked her, "Did he stop?" "Oh, no," she replied, "he kept hitting the ball the same way. But I felt so good being able to say he was wrong. I never could have said it before."

Why is this story important? Because it shows that you may not get what you want, or only part of it, but when it's over you can say to yourself, "I did what I could, I liked the way I acted, I really tried even if I didn't end up with what I wanted. Because of the way I acted I handled things. "I like me, I'm proud of the way I acted."

📄 Resource Sheet A2-2

Listening and Hearing

To understand what actually happens during a conversation, read the following.

Listening But Not Really Hearing

- A listener may stop listening because she thinks she already knows what the speaker is going to say.
- A listener often hears the beginning and end of a statement but little of what is said in the middle.
- A listener tends to ignore ideas that she disagrees with or does not understand.
- When two people are conversing, there are times when the speaker and the listener get confused ideas about what one is saying and the other is hearing.

Now look at the "How to Hear Skills" list below.

- If you choose to listen, then listen and look attentive. Look at and face the speaker while he or she is talking.
- Make a special effort to keep with the speaker if his or her remarks are lengthy.
- If the speaker goes on and on, intervene occasionally to remain involved. "Are you saying . . . ?"
- Ask for clarification when you are confused. "I'm confused about that last point" or "When you say _____, do you mean _____?"
- Respond with nods, "Yes" and "Um hmm" to encourage people to continue and indicate understanding.
- Concentrate on listening — don't reply until the speaker is finished.
- Whenever appropriate, paraphrase or summarize what you believe is the content of the speaker's message to check your understanding of what is being said. Paraphrase means putting what you think the speaker said in your own words. Here are some examples of what you might say: "If I understand you correctly . . . ", "It sounds to me like you think that . . . ," "You sound like you feel . . . "
- Don't worry if you are right or not. If not, the speaker will straighten you out.

Resource Sheet A2-3

Activity: Name That Feeling

Feelings are tellable and whatever is tellable can be more manageable. Whether we are teenagers or adults, adding to our emotional vocabulary can often add to our ability to cope with what we're feeling. Using words to describe what's inside helps remind us that what we're experiencing is human and telling our feelings to others can make those feelings more controllable.

Read the following story and in the blanks below list all the feelings you think Janelle felt. There are no right or wrong answers. You may use the list of feeling words or think of others that may not be on the list.

Janelle's Story

"I had one bad year—ninth grade—when I did everything from drinking, drugs, older guys, bad friends, you name it, mostly because I was mixed up. It just lasted a year, but I am still paying for those mistakes. Everyone remembers and still sees me as that past person.

I feel as though I will always be dragging that past around with me forever. All kinds of people still come up to my boyfriend and say "I hear Janelle drinks and smokes and is easy," and so on. But the worst thing is that every time I have any problems, I immediately think, "Maybe if I hadn't behaved like that, this wouldn't have happened.""

Feeling Words

scared	excited	happy	embarrassed	proud	sad
confused	worried	relieved	glad	put down	content
angry	lonely	in control	bored	grateful	frustrated
miserable	capable	powerful	peaceful	affectionate	loving
delighted	cool	uptight	bitter	grouchy	bold
nervous	irritated	frightened	ashamed	guilty	regretful

Janelle feels:

_____

Every feeling has a cause. Think of a situation that could cause the following feelings in you. Then how would you tell someone about it.

Feelings	**Situation**	**What I Could Say**
Lonely	_____	_____
	_____	_____
Hurt	_____	_____
	_____	_____
Terrific	_____	_____
	_____	_____
Love	_____	_____
	_____	_____

Now turn to the person on your right and tell each other the feeling, situation, and what you could say. Look her in the eyes when you talk. Notice how the same feeling can be caused by different situations. Did your feeling change (get stronger or lessen) after you spoke about it?

Resource Sheet A2-4

Activity Sheet: What Do I Like to Do?

What do you do in your spare time. For example, do you like to listen to music, dance, read draw, be outdoors, sports, play games, hang out with friends?

Draw a picture or a symbol of at least three things you like to do in the space below. Draw it any way you like, just so you know what it means. Don't draw anything fancy, we only have about five minutes to do this.

Resource Sheet A2-5

Activity Sheet: What Do I Like About Myself?

Think about what you like about yourself. What are your strengths? They could be something about your appearance, your personality, what you do well. For example, are you a good listener, are you good at a sport, have you ever won a prize, are you a good cook, can you write, are you a good student, are you a good baby-sitter, a good dancer?

Draw a picture of at least three of the things you like about yourself in the space below. After you have finished, everyone in the group will show their picture to the group and explain it. Don't worry about what it looks like, just so you know what it means.

Take your picture home and paste it on your mirror. Make sure you look at it when you get up in the morning and before you go to bed at night.

Homework

Readings
- True Story 2 – I Like Me (A2-1)
- Listening and Hearing (A2-2)

Activities
- Try your listening skills and record your reactions and results.
- Complete the exercise Getting to Your Point
- Post the compliments given to you by the others in the group on your mirror in your room and look at them before you go to bed and first thing in the morning.
- Record any thoughts or feelings in your journal.
- Give three compliments to other people and record results in journal.

📄 **Resource Sheet A2-6**

Activity Sheet: Get to Your Point*

You will help other people treat you the way you want if you can make your statements to them very specific and concrete. Being concrete means talking about *specific experiences* (what happened to you, what others do to you), *specific behaviors* (what I do), and *specific feelings* (feelings that accompany your experience and your behavior).

Telling someone "I want you to respect me" is too general to be of much help to the other person. People show respect differently. Telling yourself your goal in assertiveness training is to be treated with respect is not much help either. It is more helpful to decide what being treated with respect involves for you. For instance, it may mean "I do not want to listen to constant put-downs," or it may mean "if you cancel a date, call me and tell me instead of just not showing up," or "if you want to borrow something of mine, tell me first."

Concrete Talking About Experiences

In the following exercise, write about two experiences (what *happens* to me, what others *do* to me) first vaguely, then concretely. Look at the examples:

- **Example 1:** Vague statement of experience, " I want you to stop picking on me."
  Concrete statement: "When you call me 'Piggy' and 'Stubby' you are making fun of me and insulting me."

- **Example 2:** Vague statement of experience: "I'm not being treated right. I'm being ignored."
  Concrete statement: "Whenever I tell you my opinion, you talk right over me."

In the spaces below, write about two experiences you have had. Do not include feelings or behaviors at this point.

Vague _____

Concrete _____

_____

_____

Vague _____

Concrete _____

_____

_____

Exercises in Helping Skills, a Manual to Accompany the Skilled Helper, A Problem-Management Approach to Helping, 5th ed. by Gerald Egan. © 1994, reprinted with permission of Wadsworth, an imprint of the Wadsworth Group, a division of Thomson Learning.

Concrete Talking About Behavior (What *You* Do or Fail to Do)

- **Example 1:** Vague statement of behavior: "I messed up today."
  Concrete statement: "I hung out with friends yesterday and didn't do my homework that was due today."
- **Example 2:** Vague statement: "I got talked into doing something wrong"
  Concrete statement: I let my friends talk me into drinking at the party."

Vague _____

Concrete _____

_____

_____

Vague _____

Concrete _____

_____

_____

Concrete Talking About Feelings (Feelings Related to What *I* Do)

- **Example 1:** Vague statement: "Thanks for inviting me, but I have a hard time in groups."
  Concrete statement: "I'm not going to the group because I feel embarrassed when I can't explain what I mean."
- **Example 2:** Vague statement: "I'm bothered because we don't seem to be getting along anymore."
  Concrete statement: "I feel hurt and frustrated when you never want to listen to what I want to do."

Vague _____

Concrete _____

_____

_____

Vague _____

Concrete _____

_____

_____

Concrete Talk Bringing Experiences, Behaviors, and Feelings Together

Pick out the experiences, behaviors, and feelings in the following concrete example.

Vague statement: "People turn me off sometimes."
Concrete statement: "I feel small and stupid when my friends brag about their accomplishments. I clam up, and then I feel even worse, different, and miserable.

Experience _____

Behavior _____

Feelings _____

Now, make a vague statement about yourself and your behavior, and then change it to a concrete statement with specific experiences, behaviors, and feelings.

Vague _____

_____

Concrete _____

_____

_____

_____

Resource Sheet A2-7

Supplemental Exercise: Deeper Listening

Purpose
- To learn a more complex step in active listening.
- To communicate emphatic understanding.
- To learn how to add accurate identification of feelings to content.

Discussion
- This exercise adds "feelings" to your summarization of the message the speaker is telling you. It should follow the steps already practiced during the session.
- If you can accurately reflect both the feelings and the content of the speaker's message, the speaker will feel that not only is she being listened to but that you understand her as well. In the beginning, you will be asked to use the formula "You feel (a feeling word) because (summarize the content of the message). Later on you can translate these rather stilted words into your own language.
- An advantage to adding feeling words to your response is that it gives the speaker a chance to clarify her thinking by correcting you, if you don't get the feeling exactly right. Remember, you don't have to solve the other person's problems and you don't give advice—you are listening!

Procedure
- The leader says to the group, "Let's look at the following example. How would you respond to Megan in this scenario? How would you feel if you were in her shoes?"
    » Megan says, "Luann and Jan showed up at the party in dresses and with dates. And there I was, alone and in pants!"
- Leader asks for responses from group. There is no one correct feeling word.
  You feel _____ because _____.
- Sometimes the speaker will have more than one feeling during her message. See if you can identify both feelings.
    » Brandi says, "I got up there in front of the class, and nothing would come out. I couldn't even remember the topic of my talk. Nothing like that has ever happened to me before. I couldn't even say that nothing would come out! So I just sat down."
- You feel both _____ and _____
  because _____.
- Now let's separate into groups of two, a speaker and a listener. The speaker talks briefly about a situation that has come up or that she is facing in her real life. The listener responds with the "you feel" statements as above.
- Change roles so that each has a chance to be speaker and listener.

- Next, go through the process again but this time try to respond with feelings and a summary of the content in your own words.
- The leader gets the group together after everyone has had a turn and asks for reactions from the group. "Did they feel listened to? How did they feel about their partner?"

Discussion

- If deeper listening is to become part of your communication style, you will have to practice it in the real world. But first observe communication between people. Is it rare or common? Observe how often you use deeper listening. Next, start using deeper listening in everyday conversations. But don't be phony, use it genuinely. Observe the impact your deeper listening has upon others. What does it do for the communication process?

Resource Sheet A2-8

Supplemental Exercise: All About Me

Purpose

- To recognize each other's individuality.
- To realize that we have public and private personalities.
- To build a sense of group identity.

Materials

- Colored construction paper, magazines, personal photograph, glue, scissors, writing paper.

Discussion

- The leader explains that everyone is different in many ways. They may like to do different things, like different food, pets, hobbies, or colors.
- We are also different in what we like to show everyone about ourselves—our public self, and what we show to only a few people—our privates self.
- The leader can then show her own personal book that she has made up beforehand and explain what the pictures and items mean. One leader had a poem, a photograph of herself taken at an important time and printed words.

Procedure

- Each girl is given a piece of construction paper of her choice of color and told to fold it in half.
- She can pick pictures and words from the magazines or write messages on paper to paste on the outside of the "book" to show the public self.
- Her private self is shown on the inside of the folded paper.
- When finished, each person shares her book with the group.
- The books can be completed at home with the addition of personal photographs or written messages and brought for discussion to the next session.

Resource Sheet A3-1

Activity: My Values

Directions

Values are your beliefs. They are important to you and you base your choices, behavior and actions on these values. This is a confusing world we live in. At every turn we must choose how we will live our lives. Even getting through the day involves deciding between competing alternatives, "Should I stay home and watch TV tonight or go to a friend's house?" "Should I wear the white or blue blouse?" to more important "Do I care more about how a boy friend looks than his personality?" to "What kind of a career do I want?" To make things more complicated, values change. What you thought was important five years ago may not be important to you now. These values will keep changing. But for now it will help you to understand your actions and think about your choices if you know your values.

This exercise will give you practice in choosing among alternatives and in publicly explaining and defending them. If they are important to you, say so! Rank order your choices, with number one being your first choice.

1. Where would you rather be on a Saturday afternoon?

    ___ at the beach or park

    ___ a good friend's house

    ___ at the mall

2. Which is most important in a friendship?

    ___ loyalty

    ___ generosity

    ___ honesty

3. Which would you *least* like to be?

    ___ very poor

    ___ very sickly

    ___ disfigured

    ___ retarded

4. If you were a parent, how late would you let *your* 14 year old stay out?

    ___ 10 p.m.

    ___ 12 p.m.

    ___ it's up to him or her

5. What do you think is most harmful?

   ___ cigarettes
   ___ marijuana
   ___ alcohol
   ___ guns

6. When you worry about a mark on an exam do you think about

   ___ your self-esteem
   ___ your parents
   ___ pleasing your teacher
   ___ getting into college

7. If I gave you $500, what would you do with it?

   ___ save it
   ___ give it to charity
   ___ spend it
   ___ give some of it to a friend

📄 Resource Sheet A3-2

Activity: Personal Rights

Below is a list of rights everyone can claim. However, since you are not fully grown up and independent, you may be able to claim these rights with some groups of people, say people your own age, but not with parents or teachers. We usually deal with three groups of people, *commercial* (salesclerks, office workers), *authority* (parents, teachers, doctors, bosses) and *peers* (boy and girls your own age).

As you read the rights, think about with which groups you can claim these rights. Write down the group(s) in the blank after each right. Use their initials c, a, or p. It may be possible to use this right with more people than you think. We'll talk about that later.

- The right to say no to unreasonable requests. _____
- The right to say no to boys. _____
- The right to express my feelings, including anger—as long as I don't violate the rights of others and to experience the consequences. _____
- The right to be competitive and succeed. _____
- The right to have my needs be as important as the needs of other people. _____
- The right to decide which activities will fulfill my needs. _____
- The right to make mistakes and be responsible for them. _____
- The right to privacy. _____
- The right to have my opinions given the same respect and consideration that other people's opinions are given. _____
- The right to change my mind. _____
- The right to get what I pay for. _____
- The right to ask for information. _____
- The right to say "I don't know" and "I don't understand." _____
- The right not to make excuses for things I do. _____
- The right to decide when to be assertive. _____
- The right to ask for what I want or need _____
- Can you think of another right? _____
- Now think of a situation where you did not act assertively. Write it down.

_____
_____
_____

- What rights were involved?
  _____
  _____
  _____

 **Resource Sheet A3-3**

Activity: Everybody Has Rights

Read the scenarios below and decide which ones you would be willing to act in. They involve three different kinds of people we frequently deal with. The first is a commercial situation, the second is a peer situation, and the last is one with an authority figure.

What rights does each person in the scenarios have? Look at your list of rights for ideas. Which rights were violated?

Scenario 1

Andrea has been waiting to give her money to the cashier after choosing the perfect tee-shirt. The cashier is chatting to a friend and seems to be ignoring Andrea. Finally Andrea has lost patience and says loudly to the cashier. "Hey, how about some service here. I've been waiting forever!"

Scenario 2

Cara's friend Beth is going to try smoking cigarettes and wants Cara to join her. Cara doesn't want her friend to think she's uncool but doesn't really want to smoke. Cara says, "You shouldn't smoke, it's not healthy, it makes you stink, and I'm telling you this for your own good."

Scenario 3

Hillary's dad has just told her she is grounded for a week because she came home two hours later than she had promised. Hillary says, "But it wasn't my fault, my driver didn't want to leave. You're not being fair!"

Now think of situations where you want to be assertive with the groups listed below and write three rights these people have.

- Commercial people (salesclerk, office workers).

_____

_____

_____

- Authority (parents, teachers, doctors, bosses).

_____
_____
_____

- Peers (friends, teenagers, persons your age, boys).

_____
_____
_____

 **Resource Sheet A3-4**

Activity: The Swap Meet (Trade-offs)

Cut along the lines and separate into three piles. The first pile is trade-offs you can give up fairly easily. The second is the trade-offs that are somewhat harder to give up and possibly a third pile that may be difficult or impossible to do without.

I get protection from others.	I avoid possible conflict/anger/rejection in order to keep relationships.
I believe that others make me feel the way I do.	I must get my way.
I don't make suggestions, so I can't be considered responsible.	I will hurt their feelings and they won't like me. (I'm responsible for how others feel.)
It's too scary to try some other behaviors especially when I don't know how others will respond to me. So I will stay the same.	I don't let people know much about me, how I feel or think so I won't get hurt.
I can't make mistakes because I like being thought of as perfect. If I do, it means that I'm no good.	I put up with obnoxious behavior in order to keep my boy or girl friends.
I let others make decisions for me. Then it's never my fault if I choose wrong. (I can blame them.)	Being aggressive (letting my anger out on others) makes me feel powerful.
If I don't ask for what I want I won't be turned down.	Being sarcastic and putting others down makes me feel superior.

Resource Sheet A3-5

Activity Sheet: Observer's Check List

Check the assertive behavior shown by the role player in the appropriate space. Write suggestions for improvement in the next column. Be sure suggestions are specific and refer to behavior.

Assertive Behavior	R.P. 1	Suggestions	R.P. 2	Suggestions	R.P. 3
Body language: direct eye contact					
Erect confident posture					
Content: concise, to the point					
Appropriately assertive to the situation					
Definite and firm					
Perhaps a factual reason but no long-winded explanations, excuses, or apologies					
Stayed on track					
How soon was it said? Almost immediately					
No nervous joking or laughing					
No whining, sarcasm, or begging					

Homework

Read
📖 Misfits? (A3-6)

Activities
◎ Use "rights" won in swap meet
◎ Give three compliments to other people
◎ Continue practice using listening skills
◎ Record in diary:
  » Results of using rights won in swap meet
  » Results of giving three compliments to other people
  » Reactions from practicing listening skills
  » What have you learned about yourself?

Notes

Resource Sheet A3-6

Misfits?

- Misfits can be:
  - different
  - independent
  - ahead of the pack
  - original
- Is it okay to be a misfit or are you afraid of being one?
- We all have different gifts, so we all have different ways to say to the world who we are.

What a boring world it would be if everybody was perfect—no risks, no obstacles, no originality, and no thrills. Aren't we lucky to live in an imperfect world!

Resource Sheet A3-7

Supplemental Exercise: Additional Value Suggestions

- Which would you rather be?
___ an only child
___ the youngest child
___ the oldest child
- Which do you think more money should be spent on?
___ stopping crime in schools
___ better teachers
___ cure for AIDS
___ homeless shelters
- What would you most likely do about a person who has bad breath?
___ directly tell him or her
___ send an unsigned note
___ nothing
- What would you most like to improve?
___ your looks
___ the way you use your time
___ your social life
- Who would you go for help with a problem?
___ a friend
___ a parent
___ a teacher or counselor
___ a minister
- What's most important in picking a boyfriend?
___ what my friends think of him
___ how he looks
___ how nice he is to me
___ how popular he is
___ how smart he is
- Where would you prefer to sit in school?
___ near the window
___ near the door
___ in the front of the room

- What is hardest for you to do?

___ be quiet

___ talk in front of the group

___ talk to a teacher

- What makes you the most angry?

___ a teacher who treats you without respect

___ a friend who won't listen to your side of an argument

___ your parents telling you what to do

Resource Sheet A3-8

Supplemental Exercise: Discovering Me

Complete the sentences below. After everyone is done, we will go over the answers in the group and then discuss the last two questions.

When I am alone, I like to _____

I get embarrassed when _____

I especially like _____

I hate it when _____

I worry about _____

I am proud about _____

I want to be _____

I feel good when I _____

I need to work more on _____

Some people who mean a lot to me are _____
_____

They mean a lot because _____
_____

What did you discover about yourself?

Is there anything you can do to feel better about yourself?

Resource Sheet A3-9

Supplemental Exercise: Building Confidence

You learn something about yourself with every new experience you have tried. Think about it! Look at the examples below for some ideas and then think back over the past month or so. Have you tried anything new? What did you learn about yourself. Even if you didn't like what you tried, that taught you something. Think about sports, new friends, hobby started, a new web site discovered. If you haven't tried anything new, you're in a rut. Now's the time to do it!

- List below some of the things you tried and what you learned about yourself.
- Tell the person on either side of you what you did and what you learned.

Things I Have Tried	What I Have Learned from the Experience
Examples: Started yoga class	Discovered muscles
Discovered web site	Skill improved
Visited new place	Know more about the world

Resource Sheet A4-1

Blocks to Assertion

We do not believe we have the right.

We do not want to take the responsibility.

We use unrealistic beliefs or fears.

We lack the skills.

Resource Sheet A4-2

Activity: Bad News Beliefs

What is a Bad News Belief (BNB)? It is a belief that makes you feel bad about yourself, makes you feel like curling up in a ball and disappearing, makes your stomach feel like its sinking down into your feet.

How do you know when you are at the mercy of a Bad News Belief? Just feel into your body. That's where your emotions are. That's why, if you feel bad enough, your body can even get physically sick. Your body is not the cause of your feelings, your thoughts are. Your body just responds. If you are judging yourself, putting yourself down, or feeling jealous (which is a way of telling yourself you aren't good enough) your body will feel like it is shrinking inside or you'll feel very heavy or down, or you feel like striking out at someone or something.

So the good news is that if you feel those uncomfortable feelings inside you don't have to just sit there and feel bad. You can take an opportunity to break free into something new. Any time you feel less than great you can stop for a minute and back track. Ask yourself, "What was I just telling myself? Was I giving myself sunshine and watering myself with love? Or was I poisoning myself with negativity?"

Think of yourself as a very precious and unique flowering plant. If you want this plant to grow strong and healthy would you beat it down and feed it toxic waste? Of course not. A Bad News Belief is like toxic waste.

Contrary to popular belief, self-punishment doesn't lead to improved behavior. Beating yourself up for believing that you are not good at volleyball and comparing yourself negatively to the girls that are great at it is not going to get you motivated to practice so that you can get better at it. It's more likely to fill you so full of toxic shame that you are worse at it next time. You'll play a lot better if you can laugh it off and ask someone on your team to show you how to improve your game.

You know, when I was in school I somehow picked up the BNB that you were either born good at something or not. Beth was a good runner. I wasn't. You either knew how to draw or you didn't. You were good at math or you weren't. Somehow it didn't occur to me that these kids just had more practice or help at home than I did.

Jenny's mom was an artist and had taught her to draw. Susan had a lot of brothers to play with and spent a lot of time either running with them or from them. Jordan's dad was a math professor. I just believed that I wasn't good at those things. So I felt bad about myself and gave up instead of asking for help or practicing.

So the nugget of wisdom I'm going to pass on to you is this: Anything can be learned. If someone is better at something than you, they may have a knack for it, but most likely they've just been at it a bit longer, or are giving it more time and attention because they love it. It never pays to compare yourself to someone else. Everyone has a different purpose in life. It's like comparing a guitar to a bicycle. Which is better?

Resource Sheet A4-3

Activity: Bad News, Good News

Notice the difference between the statements below, both are referring to the same person. One statement is a judgment—a Bad News Belief (BNB). The other is an factual observation. Notice the different feeling each statement gives you:

"I am ugly," *or* "I have six zits at the moment."

"I have boring eyes," *or* "I have pale eyelashes."

"I have ugly teeth," *or* "My front teeth are crooked."

"I'm stupid," *or* "I got a C in math."

"I'm a klutz," *or* "I haven't learned those dance steps yet."

"Nobody likes me," *or* "I didn't get invited to the party for some reason that I don't know."

"I'm fat," *or* "My jeans don't fit anymore."

"I'm so uncool," *or* "My mother wouldn't let me go to the concert."

"I have a big nose," *or* "My nose is slightly larger than some of the others."

Pair up with the person sitting beside you. Write down some of the *judgments* you have about yourself in the first column. In the second column write the *factual* statement. Help each other think of factual statements. Do they help you change your feelings?

Judgments	**Factual Statements**

Now look at your factual statements. Let's make them more positive so that when you catch yourself putting yourself down, you can replace the put-down with the factual statement and then reinforce it by adding a positive statement to it. Some examples of positive statements:

- I deserve friends that are helpful and fun.
- Many kids my age have zits, I'll grow out of them, plus I have pretty eyes and a nice smile.
- I can practice with friends or take dancing lessons or I can do whatever else I want.
- I am a good friend to have and a lot of fun.

Factual Statement _____

Positive Statement (Good News Belief) _____

_____

_____

Factual Statement _____

Positive Statement (Good News Belief) _____

_____

_____

Factual Statement _____

Positive Statement (Good News Belief) _____

_____

_____

When you've filled in the blanks, the leaders will ask you to close your eyes again and imagine the same situation you did at the beginning. When you have recaptured your yucky feelings, you will be asked to start thinking of your realistic statement and your positive statement instead. Notice whether your yucky feeling changes.

The good news is that if you find yourself at the mercy of a BNB and you find yourself feeling down, you don't have to just sit there and feel bad. When you notice the yucky feeling, you can thank that yucky feeling for giving you an opportunity to bust up a BNB and break free into something new.

Each time you do this, it gets easier to do it the next time. The more you do it, the greater your self-esteem, the freer and happier and more powerful you get at playing the game of life. You'll make better choices. Not only will you be a happier person, but people will want to be around you more.

Resource Sheet A4-4

Activity: Stopping My Bad News Voice*

Think of someone putting you down and what you say to yourself in response. Give that voice in your head a name. It could be something like "Critic" or "Josephine." Write the name here. _____

Now pair up with someone you haven't paired up with before and have one of you be the bad news voice and give you put-downs. She could ask you to do something you know is wrong or don't want to do and when you refuse she starts putting you down. Or she could criticize your appearance or any behavior.

Remember, she is your own bad news voice who now has a name. So you answer with "I'm sorry you feel that way, Josephine," or "Oh, there you go again Critic, but that's not the truth," and use your positive good news belief. Your partner will continue to put you down three or four times with different criticisms and you answer each time with your bad news voice's name and your positive Good News Belief. Than you change roles and give her the business.

*Adapted from *Group Exercises for Enhancing Social Skills and Self-Esteem* (Vol. 2, pp. 75 and 77, Exercise 35–Changing My Critical Inner Voice), by S. S. Khalsa, 1999, Sarasota, Fla.: Professional Resource Press, P. O. Box 15560, Sarasota, FL 34277-1560. Copyright 1999 by Professional Resource Exchange, Inc. Adapted with permission.

Homework

Read

📖 True Story 3 – Early Warning Signals (A4-5)

Activities

◎ Record your responses to the activities below in your journal.
   » Practice imagining a stressful situation and using your Good News Beliefs (accurate plus positive statements) to calm your stressful feelings, 10 minutes each day.
   » Call on you magnificent true self whenever you need her.
   » Give two compliments, one to a friend, one to a parent.
   » Notice if someone gives you a compliment. Record your response in your journal.

◎ Find a stone or object to symbolize your magnificent true self. Paint or decorate it. Keep it with you as a reminder.

◎ Do the relaxation exercise before you go to sleep each night.

Resource Sheet A4-5

True Story 3 – Early Warning Signals

When I was 17, I decided to move out of my parents house and get my own place before I went off to college. It was the early 70's and all of my friends smoked pot and did other stuff like LSD, peyote, and cocaine. Fortunately no one I was close to did heroin, and I had heard enough about what it did to people to have a healthy fear of having anything to do with it or anything that had to do with needles. But a lot of kids were into pot and cocaine without seeming to get irrevocably messed up. What I didn't know was that the people supplying cocaine and a lot of people (not friends of mine) who used it were really hard core, that is "not friendly" and dangerously "not normal."

When I went to visit my brother who was in college, I was introduced to a friend of some hippies, who imported drugs. They were older and very hip, and I thought they were totally cool. I though it would be cool to bring some drugs back so I could turn on my friends and make a few bucks on the side. Since I had never done this before and since they were definitely much cooler than I was, I was really nervous. Half paralyzed with terror might have been more accurate. The truth is, if I had known better, I would have seen the red warning flags waving. But I didn't. I was afraid of them and afraid of seeming young and stupid.

So I returned home with my small amount of cocaine, ready for use and sale. What I didn't know was that my downstairs neighbors (who *really* gave me the creeps), **red flag, red flag,** were hard-core junkies. They bought the coke from me and shot it up. The next day they came upstairs and demanded their money back because they said it wasn't any good. (What did I know about the quality of stuff you shoot up?) I think I was only able to give them part of the money back so they were pretty pissed off. A couple of nights later they stole my bicycle (a 10-speed English racer that was my whole life) and sold it. I couldn't prove anything and although I called the police, I never saw that bike again. I was heartbroken. But the truth is I got off easy.

A few years later, while at college, I saw the guy that sold me the "bad" coke walking down the street. This time he *really* gave me the creeps. He was a walking skeleton, his skin looked gray and he had a big, ugly red scar cutting across his throat from ear to ear, where it looked like someone had tried to slit it. I walked by really fast.

You know, that could have been me. Although I still mourn the loss of that incredible bike, I feel I was really lucky. It was a big price to pay but I didn't have to pay for it with my life or any part of my body.

So although a lot of times fear is there to be overcome, sometimes it is our friend, our inner warning device that says, "Girlfriend! What are you doing? Get out of there!" For me, it feels like my stomach and throat tighten up, like my insides are shrinking and taking a few steps backwards. What is it like for you?

Resource Sheet A4-6

Activity: My True Self*

Now is the time to start thinking about who your real self is. During this coming week, spend some time getting in touch with the true self you experienced in this session. You can do this simply by feeling in your heart where your true self lives, by saying her name and listening and feeling for her. It is a place deep inside where you can go and no one can follow you, no one can hurt you, and no one can change you. It is the angel inside of all of us. Everyone has this special place.

- Find a stone or special object. This will be a symbol for your true self.
- Paint it your favorite color, or draw a picture on it that reflects your true self. Do you think of yourself as a flower waiting to blossom? Or are you a small plant or tree struggling to grow? Maybe you are a song or a poem or a story.
- When you look at it, it will remind you of that special place. Even if you can't see it, or aren't holding it, you can imagine it glowing deep inside of you.
- As you go through the week look inside for your magnificent true self and imagine that the glow or dullness transfers itself to your stone. Watch your stone glow or get dull.
- What would make your stone shine brightly? What would make your stone become dull?
- When you come back next week, tell the others about your stone or object and what happened to it during the week.

---

*Reprinted from *Girls Speak Out: Finding Your True Self* by Andrea Johnston. © 1997 by Andrea Johnson. Reprinted by permission of Scholastic Inc.

Resource Sheet A4-7

Supplemental Activity: Getting Rid of Toxic Waste

Are you thinking of yourself as a toxic waste field where nothing will grow? You're right! Until you dig up the toxic waste—your Bad News Beliefs—and throw them away, the precious, flowering plant you want to become, will not grow. So, write down your BNBs about each topic below until you feel you have really dug them out of your mind. Then crumple up the paper and throw it in the waste basket. After all, that's what waste is, something that can be thrown away.

- Family
  _____
  _____
  _____

- Friends
  _____
  _____
  _____

- School
  _____
  _____
  _____

- My Body
  _____
  _____
  _____

- Work
  _____
  _____
  _____

- Love
  _____
  _____
  _____

- Anything left in there?
  _____
  _____
  _____

Resource Sheet A4-8

Supplemental Exercise: Learning to Listen to Your Early Warning Signals

Purpose

To identify, clarify, and strengthen participants' intuitive, warning signals so that they can recognize potential trouble and avoid it or take the appropriate action.

Discussion

After reviewing Early Warning Signals (A4-5), think about a time when you got into a negative situation, or something yucky happened to you. Try to pick something that wasn't absolutely horrific, but something you can handle dealing with in this group. Were there any clues before it happened that you ignored, that, when you look back, if you had listened, might have helped you to do something differently?

Visualization

Now close your eyes and allow yourself to imagine going back in time to just before the event. Perhaps you can imagine or allow yourself to dream up what it really felt like then . . . How old were you? . . . Were you alone or were there others around? . . . Who was there? . . . What was happening? . . . What were you feeling? . . . What did you feel like in your body?

Allow yourself to remember what you were thinking about. Allow yourself to become aware of any cues or clues that maybe something was not quite right . . . What were those cues? Were the cues something that you heard, saw, felt in your body, or just knew somehow?

Allow yourself to go through the whole event in your mind while paying attention to your body and the warning signals it gives you. (Pause for a few minutes.) When you feel ready, just bring yourself back to the room. When you open your eyes, go ahead and write down those cues or warning signals in you journal.

Discussion

Was anyone able to pick up any early warning cues before the event occurred? What did you notice? Were the cues something you heard, saw, felt, or just knew? Did you notice any changes in the feelings in your bodies as they went through the event? How do you experience the feeling of something being "creepy" or "wrong" or "scary." How could you use this information in the future. What could you have done differently if you had listened to the warning.

Visualization

Now, close your eyes again and imagine going back to just before the negative event occurred. Put yourself back in time . . . allowing yourself to really dream yourself there . . . thinking the same thoughts, feeling the same feelings . . . only now, when you get that first warning signal, imagine yourself paying attention to it . . . and this time . . . doing something differently. See, feel, and imagine what changes. Notice how you feel. (Allow a minute or two of quiet.)

Now, when you feel ready, bring yourself back to the room. When you open your eyes, just spend a few minutes writing about what was different this time.

Discussion

What was different? How did it feel to listen to the messages you were receiving? How did it feel to act on those messages? How could you use this information in the future? In what kinds of situations could this information be useful?

📄 **Resource Sheet A5-1**

Activity Sheet: Peer Pressure

Your friends' influence or peer pressure can be uncomfortable, especially if it is something that feels bad to you, something that goes against what you feel is right, something that might feel good at the time but could have negative consequences in your life. That is, could it affect your body, your self-worth, your future. For instance, taking drugs can ruin your life by killing you, messing up your mind permanently, or you ending up in prison which prevents you from having a successful life.

Below is a picture of a girl representing you. All around her are her friends pushing her to do something. Under each situation, write possible negative pressures you can feel from them. After you have heard everyone's peer pressures, check one that you will use to work on next.

Boys	**Girls**
At school	At school
At parties	At parties
At the mall	At the mall
In homes	In homes
At the movies	At the movies
On public transportation	On public transportation

Anywhere or anything else

Resource Sheet A5-2

Activity Sheet: I'm in Control

☑ **Why does this make you feel uncomfortable, what is your value or belief?**

☑ **What could be the consequences?**

☑ **This is what I choose to do instead for my best welfare.**

☑ **This is what I will tell them.**

☑ **I will stick to my decision.**

Example

- Situation–some of your friends want you to go to the mall and help them shoplift.
- You believe stealing is wrong.
- If we get caught, it's not worth the public humiliation and could wreck my life.
- You choose to refuse to go with them.
- Tell them the reason for your decision, "I won't go to the mall with you because I am uncomfortable taking things that don't belong to me. The consequences if we get caught aren't worth it."
- If they keep insisting, I will just leave.

Write below the situation you want to work on from the peer-pressure activity sheet.

Situation:
_____

Why does this make you feel uncomfortable, what is your value or belief?
_____

What could be the consequences if you went along with the pressure?
_____

This is what I choose to do instead for my best welfare.
_____

This is what I will tell them.
_____

How I will stick to it.
_____

You can work out other situations the same way so that when or if they come up you will be prepared with an answer.

Resource Sheet A5-3

Activity: Combining Broken Record With Understanding and Reaching a Workable Compromise

Separate into groups of three and decide who will be the *asserter*, the *coach* and the *requester*. Each of you will take turns playing each role in this exercise. The asserter may be helpful, but it is not her responsibility to solve the other person's problems. Repeat over and over your basic message of refusal. Remember how a manipulator operates. Do not forget to be understanding. Try a workable compromise if the request is important or if you wish to practice. The coach may help the asserter keep to the basic message and/or help the requester manipulate.

The requester can ask the asserter to refuse a request such as borrowing something, fund raising for the school band, joining a club, or a friend asking for help babysitting a pet. Other situations can be: mother-daughter relationships, boyfriend-girlfriend relationships, situations involving friends or other relatives, or pick a situation from your own experience. Follow the steps below.

Combining Broken Record with Understanding

Step 1. Their position (understanding)

Step 2. Your position (explanation)

Step 3. Action (your message)

Example: "I can see how you really need the money . . . but I just don't have any that I can spare right now . . . I'm sorry but I can't lend you anything.

Example: "I realize you're in a tight spot . . . but I'm very busy myself right now . . . so I'm really sorry but I won't be able to help you right now." With a workable compromise, add, "I will have some time on Monday if you can wait," or "Can we work something else out?"

Homework

Read
- True Stories 4 (A5-4)
- Helpful Hints for Saying "No" to Unfair Requests and Demands (A5-5)

Activities
- Practice refusing unreasonable requests and record reactions in your journal.
- Become aware of how you handle criticism and record reactions in your journal.
- How did you handle the complements you received? Record in your journal.
- Give two compliments. Record how they were received and how you did in your journal.
- What does your "true-self rock" look like now? Record your journal.
- Write a short paragraph or two describing your "true self." Bring it to the next session to share if you wish. There are some examples on Resource Sheet 5-4.

Resource Sheet A5-4

True Stories 4*

Read the samples of true stories written by other girls. After you have read the true stories, you can write about who you are in that special place deep inside of you that no one else knows. Write about what you have or haven't discovered so far. Bring your stories to the next session and we will share them with each other.

My Nosy Self by Alicia, 12

My true self doesn't want to be bugged yet. She's taking a nap. But when she wakes up, I think she will be adventurous and want to find out things, even scary stuff.

My True Self? by Melanie, 15

I am still uncertain about my true self. I spend most of my time studying so I can be somebody important. I think I am something one minute and something else another minute. I mean I am quiet sometimes and talkative sometimes, selfish and giving. I am lots of things, good and bad. The trouble is I listen to people's troubles so much, I don't have time to think about only me. I always feel I should be doing something to help others. I'm feeling like I'm being used up from listening to everybody. What about me? Am I really being selfish? I really never thought about my true self before but now I want to know.

I Am Special by Micheala, 14

Some people think I'm weird because I like to dress different and do strange things. But I like to be different. It makes me feel free. I think the other girls secretly admire me and wish they could be like me. I like to draw when I'm by myself and think and write. I'm a good dancer. I guess that's called being creative. Although sometimes I am lonely. I don't want to be like everyone else.

The Real Me by Anlyn, 17

I feel that I am a very kind and caring friend. Although I have always been thought to be generous, I feel that many people take me for granted. Because of this I often feel drained because I can't always please people and when I need my space, my friends don't seem to understand that it isn't personal. I think that I am very intelligent and perceptive. I truly enjoy laughing and having fun. In fact, I believe that the most beautiful noise in the world is laughter. I love to do crazy things like bungee jumping and trying anything adventurous. Despite being spontaneous, I am very cautious with my emotions and keep my feelings guarded (especially with the opposite sex). Well, I guess that somewhat sums me up.

---

*Reprinted from *Girls Speak Out: Finding Your True Self* by Andrea Johnston. © 1997 by Andrea Johnson. Reprinted by permission of Scholastic Inc.

My True Self by Chelsea, 18

    I think that at the heart of my true self, there is an ability to adapt in order to survive. Life has thrown some pretty hard times my way, and through it all, I have found an inner strength. Although I am a hard and honest worker, I think I lack patience which has often caused me grief. I do feel I have a great ability to love and to show affection, which is why I feel that my friends and family are the most important part of my life. I read once that the Sagittarius mantra is "My heart seeks truth," and I completely identify with this. In conclusion, as long as I feel I am growing as a person, I do not fear life's confusion. It has taken a long time, but I feel I do like who I am.

Resource Sheet A5-5

Helpful Hints for Saying "No" to Unfair Requests and Demands

- First be sure whether you want to say "yes" or "no." If you are not sure, explain that you need time to think it over and will let the person know when you have the answer.
- Ask for clarification if you do not fully understand what is being requested.
- Be as brief as possible. Give a legitimate reason for your refusal, but avoid long elaborate explanations and justifications. Such excuses may be used by the other person to argue you out of your "no."
- Use the word "no" or "I've decided not to . . ." when declining. Both have more power and are less uncertain than "Well, I just don't think so" and makes clear that you have made a choice.
- Make your nonverbal gestures mirror your verbal message. Shake your head when saying "no." Often people unknowingly nod and smile when they are trying to refuse.
- You may have to decline several times before a person hears you. It is not necessary to come up with a new explanation each time. Just repeat your "no" and your original reason. Remember persistence and the broken-record technique.
- If a person persists even after you have said "no" several times, use silence or change the subject.
- You may want to acknowledge the other person's feelings about your refusal, "I know this will be a disappointment for you but I won't be able to."
- Avoid feeling guilty. It is not up to you to solve other people's problems or make them happy. They can only make themselves happy.
- If you do not wish to agree to the person's original request but still desire to help, offer a compromise such as, "I will not be able to babysit the whole afternoon, but I can for two hours.
- You may have to change your mind and say "no" to a request to which you originally agreed. That is your right. Say "I know I agreed to do this, but after I thought it over, I've decided I can't."

Activities

- Practice refusing unreasonable requests and record reaction in your journal.
- Become aware of how you handle criticism and record reactions in your journal.
- How did you handle the compliments you received? Record in journal.
- Give two compliments. Record how they were given and received in your journal.
- What is your "true-self" rock looking like?
- Write one or two short paragraphs describing your "true self." Bring to the next session to share if you wish.

Resource Sheet A5-6

Supplemental Exercise:
Negotiating or Reaching a Workable Compromise

Using the scenario below, negotiate a solution using some of the skills you learned, listening, expressing opinions, rights and values, and working things out. One person can play A, another play B, and if you are in groups of three, a third can be the coach/observer. How can you work things out if you were B? The scenario can be replayed with different people taking the roles or if one of the players is having a difficult time playing a role, someone else can jump in and play the role. If you wish, try another scenario of a different situation.

Scenario

- A and B have been fooling around together at a party. Both have been drinking rather heavily. They have been slow dancing and making out on the dance floor.

- Role A: Wants to leave the party and go out to someone's car where they can have more privacy.

- Role B: Likes the attention of A and doesn't want to lose it, but is absolutely uneasy with being alone with A in the back seat of someone's car.

 **Resource Sheet A5-7**

Supplemental Exercise: Keeping the Peace

Do your parents freak out over some of your friends? Can you figure out how to handle this? This is what parents say sets them off.

- **Weird looks or vibes.** Weird hair, bizarre clothes, lots of piercing and/or tattoos, or maybe they are picking up signals or seeing inappropriate behavior.
- **Too worldly.** Your friends may be doing things your parents think you can't handle yet, such as date or stay out late. Bad influence.
- **Attitude.** Many parents don't like their kid's friends to be rude or treat others unfairly. It may rub off on you.
- **Sudden change.** If one of your friends suddenly shaves his or her hair or starts wearing all black or starts using lots of swear words, your parents can think, "Is this rebellion? Is this what my daughter thinks too?"

List below some of the things that upset your parents about your friends? They can be some of the things listed above or others that you think of.

_____

_____

_____

Now its your turn. There really are ways to do this without sulking or dropping your pal. One is to talk things over either with your parents or with your friend or with both. For example, tell your parents why you feel your friend is a good person. But be honest with yourself. If you realize that he or she makes you uncomfortable, gets you in situations over your head, ask yourself why you have picked him or her as your friend. But if you feel you are right, stick with your decision and explain using the skills learned in this session.

Below list some of the ways you can either talk to your parents or talk to your friends or otherwise handle the situations you listed.

_____

_____

_____

_____

Now try out your solutions on two or three others in your group. Ask them what they think and how you might improve on them. Remember the rules of assertiveness—respecting your rights and the other person's rights, using "I" language, listening, compromising, and ending up with both sides feeling good.

After everyone has had a turn and talked about what happened, you are ready to try it on your parents or your friend. You might want to write about it in your journal and tell your group what happened in the next session.

Resource Sheet A6-1

Activity: Admitting Mistakes

It takes guts to go to a friend and say "I was wrong," "I apologize," or "I'm sorry." It's especially hard to admit you were wrong to your parents, because, of course, you know so much more than they do. You may be surprised, though, when you do. It means a lot to them and they are the most forgiving people on earth.

- When you have made a mistake, the assertive way to handle it is to admit it. Not only do you defuse the criticism, but you also gain respect from others by being honest and responsible.
- You have a right to make mistakes, no one is perfect. You take responsibility not only by admitting that you made a mistake and saying you are sorry but also by recognizing what the other person is feeling because of your mistake.
- Show empathy. Empathy means putting yourself in the other person's shoes. "How would I feel if this happened to me?"
- The form of your apology goes something like this: "I did it. I'm sorry. You must be feeling very (irritated, upset, angry) with me. How can I make up for it?" The conversation can then go on to a more constructive discussion about how to correct the mistake.
- You can give one simple explanation for your mistake if you like, but if you go on and on about it, you will sound like you want the other person to feel sorry for you, that it's not your fault, and there is no reason for them to feel that way. A dead end will result with bad feelings on both sides— your guilt, their anger.

Procedure

Choose one of the situations below and practice admitting a mistake with your partner. Look at your partner and practice using the form suggested—"I did it. I'm sorry. You must be feeling very (irritated, upset, angry) with me. How can I make up for it?"

- You have made a date to meet your best friend at the mall and arrive 20 minutes late.
- You have borrowed a book from your teacher and lost it.
- You borrowed the family car and got in an accident.
- You are pregnant and must tell your parents.
- You hurt a friend's feelings by saying something about them that you didn't know was a secret.
- Use an experience of your own.

After the apology, ask your partner how she felt. How did you feel? Was there any way you could have apologized better?

Resource Sheet A6-2

Activity: Expressing Feelings and Needs Assertively

Assertion training emphasizes not blaming or ridiculing the other person. When you start your conversation with the word "you" as in "you did this," or "you made me," the other person feels attacked and their first impulse is to fight back rather than listen. Before you know it you are in an argument rather than working out a problem. Helpful criticism focuses on specific behavior rather than what the person is or is not.

The four-step model below is especially effective in expressing feelings, both positive and negative, in asserting rights or asking for favors.

"I" Language

Step 1. "I . . . " This is where you describe how the other person's behavior affects your behavior or feelings. If your behavior is not affected, you may be dealing with a difference in values (their beliefs). You still have the right to express your feelings, but will need to consider the other person's rights of values.

Step 2. "When . . . " You describe as factually as possible the specific behavior that either pleases or troubles you.

Step 3. "I feel . . . " You describe your present feelings. Leave this part out if it's not appropriate as in some commercial situations.

Step 4. "I'd like . . . " You describe what you want to do about the problem if it is appropriate to the situation.

- Now we will try different ways of expressing ourselves first so that we can actually see how using "you" instead of "I" affects us.
- Divide into pairs and take turns dealing with one of the situations listed below. First, try it with the word "you." Then, do it again but this time use the steps above. You can also use a situation you may be facing in your life.
  - » Ask someone to quiet down.
  - » Tell someone he or she did not do his or her share.
  - » Ask someone for a ride home, because the guy you came with is drunk.
  - » Your date has taken you to an expensive restaurant and show and now thinks he is entitled to have sex in return.
  - » Your boyfriend won't stop pressuring you to use drugs.
  - » Your boyfriend loses his temper a lot and you want to break up with him.

» You're at a slumber party and the girls are deciding to play a mean and hurtful trick on another girl. You don't think it's right.

- How did it feel starting with a "you" statement?
- How did it feel being spoken to with a "you" statement?
- How about when you used the four steps?

Resource Sheet A6-3

Activity: Keeping Your Cool (Diversion)

> "You're right, I'm sorry."
> "Yes, that's probably true."
> "That could be true."
> "I can see how you might think that."

Divide into new groups of three and act out the following roles:

- Diverter: responds to all criticism with any of the above statements and *only* the above.
- Attacker: criticizes everything about the diverter's appearance—clothing, posture, facial expression, hair style, manner of speaking, etc.
- Coach: helps diverter respond with one of the four responses, then, as the attacker runs out of criticism, switches to helping the attacker think of barbs.

How to Respond

- Now, practically every statement of criticism has some truth to it. Your response is to agree to whatever part is true. For example, "You made a mistake!" or "You got tomato sauce all over my blouse!" you respond with only "You're right, I'm sorry."
- If it is true in principle or reasoning, e.g., "If you stay out late every night, you'll get sick," you respond with "That could be true."
- If the odds are that it might be true, e.g., "Anybody who believes that must be simple minded," you respond with, "That could be true."
- If you can't agree to any part of the criticism, you respond with, "I can see how you might think that."

Reminders

- Diversion is *not* assertive and has only limited value. It is like protective armor you use while you decide how to respond.
- It is also a technique to use with people who will not listen, who argue for the sake of arguing, or with whom you have tried to be assertive and failed.
- Diversion protects you from people who think their values are better than yours, those who are not interested in hearing your side and only want to wear you down.
- It is useful only as a last resort—to shut off further argument.

Homework

Read

- Helpful Hints for Dealing With Criticism or Anger (A6-4)
- Helpful Hints for Expressing Dissatisfaction (A6-5)
- Helpful Hints for Disagreeing (A6-6)
- True Story 5 – Do You Act or React? (A6-7)

Activities

- Bring to next session What Would You Say? (A6-8)
- Start a joke collection and bring it to the next session.
- Record in your journal any attempts at assertive behavior.
- Offer to help someone; carry groceries, cut the grass, shovel snow, walk a dog, babysit. Record your reactions and feelings in your journal.
- Keep track of your "true-self" rock

Resource Sheet A6-4

Helpful Hints for Dealing With Criticism or Anger

- Relax and allow yourself to listen carefully to what the other person is saying. Breathing deeply may help you to relax.
- Summarize the criticism so that the person knows you really heard and understood the point.
- Ask for clarification if the criticism is vague or unclear, e.g., "You are rude." Ask for specific examples.
- Decide whether the criticism is fair or unfair. Question the fairness rather than the criticism.
- If it is fair criticism, ask for specific suggestions or alternatives such as what you might do to deal with the situation or behave differently.
- Do not go into long, self-critical or rationalizing excuses.
- If you disagree, respond with an opinion statement using "I" rather than "you." For example, "I think you may have misunderstood what I said," rather than "You misunderstood me."
- When responding to someone who is speaking loudly, and at a fast pace, keep your voice lower and speak slowly.
- It can be helpful to share your feelings about the criticism. For example, "It's not easy for me to take criticism."

When criticism is:	Technique to use is:
True	Admit the mistake directly
Vague	Ask for specifics
Not true	Simple direct denial

Resource Sheet A6-5

Helpful Hints for Expressing Dissatisfaction

- If you are bringing up an issue that has taken place some time ago, ask permission. Set aside a time and place. "I'd like to discuss something that has been bothering me. Do you have some time now?" or "When would be a good time?"
- Be specific and give examples. Cite situations.
- Use personal pronouns. Express your dissatisfaction without blaming, "It bothers me when you say . . . " or "I feel uncomfortable when . . . "
- Avoid name calling.
- Assume assertive body language. Be serious.
- Give some suggestions, provide ideas. "I think it's fun to trade clothes, but lately mine have been returned dirty and messed up. I would really like it if you would take better care of my stuff, if we are going to continue trading."
- Do not let negative feelings pile up until you explode. Deal with them as they happen. Do not overload the person with criticism.
- Avoid being sidetracked. When people are uncomfortable giving and receiving criticism, they will avoid the issue by changing the subject or bringing up the past. Go back to the point.

Resource Sheet A6-6

Helpful Hints for Disagreeing

- Acknowledge the other person's point of view. "I see your point, but I still think . . . " or "It sounds like this is important to you but . . . "
- Use an expanded opinion statement to express your point of view. "I just can't accept your opinion because . . . "
- Avoid name calling.
- Point out this is an opinion, not a fact. People have differing opinions and they can change. "I understand your opinion, my is different from yours. I believe . . . "
- Take some time to collect your thoughts if you need to. "I want to think about that for a minute."
- You have a right to your opinion without having to back it up with facts and figures. "According to what I've read . . . " or "I don't generally trust statistics, but my opinion is . . . " or "It is my belief that . . . "
- If you can, share your previous experience with the other person. "I used to share your opinion, but my experience has been . . . "

 **Resource Sheet A6-7**

Activity: What Would You Say?

In each of the scenarios below you are being asked to respond in an assertive way. Remember your rights, remember the other person's rights. Be specific, be assertive, listen, and use "I" language.

Scenario 1: At a restaurant, the food you ordered arrives cold. You call the server over and say:

_____

_____

Scenario 2: You are returning a pair of leggings you bought that are too small.

_____

_____

_____

Scenario 3: Your friends are teasing you about being a vegetarian.

_____

_____

_____

Scenario 4: Your best friend has kept you waiting once again for over half an hour.

_____

_____

_____

Scenario 5: You have turned in the best paper you have ever written in your life. The words just seemed to write themselves. You are shocked when the teacher returns it with the notation that she is sure you copied it and wants to see you after class.

_____

_____

_____

Scenario 6: Your boyfriend, for the third time, called at the last minute to say he couldn't meet you tonight, something else has come up.

_____

_____

_____

Scenario 7: Some of your friends are discussing who they will support for class president, at the same time making fun of the person you support and think is great.

Resource Sheet A6-8

True Story 5 – Do You Act or React?

I went with my friend, a Quaker, to a fast food take-out the other day where she bought her usual sandwich, thanking the server politely. The server didn't even acknowledge it.

"A crabby person isn't he?" I commented. "Oh, he's that way every day," shrugged my friend. "Then why do you continue to be so polite to him?" I asked. "Why not," inquired my friend. "Why should I let him decide how I'm going to act?"

It is important to know that you can't control other people's behavior. Sometimes no matter how sensible and pleasant you are, the other person may continue to be unreasonable, unpleasant, angry in return. Even if your solution to a problem is reasonable, others may not accept it. So, know that the only person you can control is yourself. You can decide how you want to behave and react and feel. It is your choice to let yourself get more or less upset by how other people behave. You are in command of your own conduct.

On the other hand, the natural reaction for almost all persons to behave when they feel they are being attacked is to fight back. That's why you can avoid this if your responses and remarks are "I" statements rather than blame sounding "you" statements. And don't forget to use humor!

Fun With Jokes

You're doing something right if you enjoy kidding around, cracking jokes, or seeing the funny side of things. Everybody enjoys a laugh. If you help them do that then you become valuable to them. One of the best things you can do is laugh. It makes you stronger. That doesn't mean you have to go around giggling all day long. Sometimes it's hard to find anything to laugh about. But if you can manage not to lose your sense of humor, you can get through some rough times. What's not funny? Being sarcastic or making fun of someone else. That's being aggressive in an underhanded way that ends up hurting people and spoiling friendships. Most important, laughter is a real survival skill. Don't let anyone tell you different.

Resource Sheet A6-9

Supplemental Activity: Feeling Good Ideas

Read the following ideas for helping yourself feel good and also raising your self-esteem. Turn to the person on your left and discuss each suggestion. Check one or two ideas to practice during the week.

- ☐ Offer to help someone carry groceries, cut grass, shovel snow, or run an errand.
- ☐ Spend some time with your younger sister or brother.
- ☐ Learn to ask for what you want.
- ☐ Don't put down yourself or anyone else.
- ☐ Before going to sleep at night, think two positive thoughts about yourself.
- ☐ Look in the mirror every morning and tell yourself three things you like about yourself.
- ☐ Before going to bed at night, think of two things you got done that day.
- ☐ Write down one thing you'd like to change about yourself. Then do it.
- ☐ Don't hang out with anyone who is always negative and complains about everything.
- ☐ Do something nice for your mom or dad.
- ☐ Try something that scares you then give yourself a reward when you do it.
- ☐ Become active in a sport. Join a team.
- ☐ Join a karate class. Even uncoordinated kids can do it.

Supplemental Exercise: Giving Criticism "Sandwiching"

Sandwiching is a way of giving constructive criticism that is assertive, uses "I" statements, and gets your message across in a nonthreatening way. You start with a positive statement, followed by your criticism, then with your positive suggestion for a solution and finally end with another positive statement.

Example: "I've always enjoyed eating here, the food is so well cooked, but this fish tastes spoiled to me. I'd like to order something else. I do want to enjoy my dinner here tonight as usual."

Example: "I've enjoyed being your friend, you are so much fun but I really felt betrayed when you told Allison I was going to break up with Jonah. Please don't tell my secrets to anyone, I want to be able to trust you because I do enjoy being with you."

How would you express your criticism or your wishes with sandwich statements?

Tonya loves to go dancing, but her boyfriend, Randy keeps taking her to the movies.

_____

_____

Luann's mom has mistakenly blamed her for starting an argument with her sister and has docked her allowance.

_____

_____

Hillary's boyfriend has been drinking too much at parties and getting loud and obnoxious.

_____

_____

📄 **Resource Sheet A7-1**

Activity: Starting Conversations or the Game of Catch

Write some ways you can start a conversation with someone in the situations below. Then pick two situations from the chalkboard or newsprint that you might find a little difficult. Write down some ways to have a conversation in these situations as well.

Example: Waiting in line at the movies; ask what he or she has heard about it.

After everyone is finished, pick one to role play. The group will help you by discussing the most appropriate behavior. Then re-enact the role play with their suggestions.

Always greet the other person with a smile and/or a handshake and say your name if you have never met before.

- At a party _____
  _____
- Being introduced to your friend's parents _____
  _____
- Making a new student feel welcome _____
  _____
- Situation _____
  _____
- Situation _____
  _____

Helpful Hints

- You begin with a simple, "Hi, my name is _____," then pause and let that person introduce him or herself. Then listen. If you don't catch the name and a lot of people don't because they are thinking of what they will say next, ask the person to spell it. Names are important to people and they are flattered that you care enough to get it right.
- After the introduction, you toss out the ball again by asking a question or making a comment about your surroundings or what's happening right then. "I wonder why this line is so long," or "What do you think of the band," or "How do you know the hostess?"
- To keep the conversation going, avoid questions that can be answered by a simple "yes" or "no" or with a single word. And do your part by tossing the ball back with a new question or statement.
- These are dropping the ball questions and statements: "Do you like this band?" "Yes." "I heard that new math teacher is really hard." "Oh, really." "Is there a Coke machine around here?" "I don't know."
- These are catching the ball and tossing it back questions and statements: "The band's okay, I like their selections but I think the bass isn't very good. What do you think?"

"Oh, really? Where did you hear that the math teacher is hard?" "I don't know where the Coke machine is. I haven't seen one. Let's look farther down the hall."

- Of course you show you are interested by your body language. Keep your eyes on the person, lean forward, and smile.
- If you start a conversation with someone and you don't get good listening cues, it doesn't necessarily mean she or he doesn't want to talk, maybe she or he is unskilled in making conversation.

Resource Sheet A7-2

Activity: Ending Conversations

If you want to develop a friendly relationship with whomever your have been talking with, you can't abruptly end the conversation. For example, the person has just said he thinks the class president has done a lousy job and you say, "See you, I have to go meet my mother." He will probably think he has offended you.

Warn the person ahead of time if you need to leave so that he or she can add a last minute comment. Then, tell the person in some way that you enjoyed talking and finally, if you wish, say that you would like to get together again soon.

Show that you enjoyed talking to the person:

- Comment on a particular thing that was said: "Thanks, I won't forget about what you said about how to track down the stuff I need for my paper." Or, "That joke you told me about the lawyer was really good, I'll have to remember to tell my dad."

- If you really want to continue the relationship, make definite plans to meet again, exchange telephone numbers, offer the person a ride home, or mention your plans for the weekend and ask the person to join you.

Pick a situation from the preceding activity sheet and think of how you want to end the conversation. Role play the situation and this time add an ending. Ask for reactions from the group and replay the situation adding their suggestions.

Situation: _____

Ending: _____

_____

Resource Sheet A7-3

Activity: Behavior Rehearsal With Muscle

Think of a situation in which you have difficulty acting assertively and complete the activity sheet. It may be a situation that you are facing soon, something you have listed as being difficult in your presession self-assessment, or a situation you feel you didn't handle well in the past.

Write a short concise description of the situation: _____
_____
_____
_____

What is my objective? (What do I want to happen?) _____
_____
_____
_____

What are my rights? _____
_____

What are the rights of the other person? _____
_____

What might be stopping me? Bad News Beliefs? What are they? How can I replace them?

Bad News Beliefs	**Good News Beliefs**
_____	_____
_____	_____
_____	_____

What can I use to reduce my anxiety? _____
_____

What do I want to say to let the other person know I hear and understand him or her?
_____
_____

What do I say to let the other person know how I feel? _____
_____

How do I tell him or her what I want? (Remember "I" language.") _____
_____
_____

Resource Sheet A7-4

Activity: Aftereffects

Well, we can't stop now, just when you've gotten started on the road to strength and higher self-esteem. This last activity will help you set some goals for yourself so that you can continue to apply what you've learned so far.

Procedure

- Think of an area you would like to improve. That is your goal, but consider if it is realistically attainable with the proper effort. Is it a reflection of your real feelings or is it an expectation of others?
- Use the examples below as guidelines to follow. Start with your idea. Then translate that into a specific behavior.

Example: I'd like to feel better about myself.

Specific behavioral goal: I will consider requests and refuse them if they are unreasonable and I don't care to do what is asked.

Least threatening	→ to →	→ Most threatening
Baby step 1: I will tell a door-to-door salesperson that I am not interested in what she is selling.	Baby step 2: I will turn down a request from Chelsea to borrow my earrings.	Baby step 3: I will refuse a date with Brian.	Baby step 4: I will break up with Josh.

- Decide on at least four situations (baby steps) you can practice working toward your goal and arrange them into steps from easiest to most threatening. Baby step #1 should be attainable with only slight anxiety.

Idea: _____

Specific behavior goal: _____

Baby step #1: _____

Baby step #2 _____

Baby step #3 _____

Baby step #4 _____

What reward can I give myself for achieving each step?

_____
_____
_____
_____

If I need support, who will I call? _____

Resource Sheet A7-5

Activity: Post-Session Self-Assessment

Identify how comfortable you feel in each of the areas listed on the post-session self-assessment sheet. If there are other areas you added to your presession self-assessment sheet, add them to the boxes at the end of the grid.

Again identify the types of people you have trouble with, for example, you may feel comfortable asking for a favor from your parents but not from boy friends. If that is so, in each column put (b) for boys, (g) for girls, (p) for parents, or (t) for teachers. Since this sheet will only be seen by you, just fill it out so that you will understand.

Compare this with the presession self-assessment to see how you improved.

Assertive Skill	Comfortable	Need More Practice	Uncomfortable
Saying "no"			
Asking for favors			
Making requests			
Expressing positive feelings			
Expressing negative feelings			
Giving compliments			
Receiving compliments			
Giving constructive criticism			
Receiving constructive criticism			
Expressing opinions			
Meeting new people			
Starting conversations			
Continuing conversations			
Talking about yourself			
Admitting mistakes			
Apologizing when at fault			
Handling other people's anger			
Expressing needs			
Asking for information from clerks			
Asking for information from teachers			
Asking for help			
Asking for explanations			

Homework

Read
- Reminder: Step by Step to Responsible Assertion (A7-6)
- What Life is All About (A7-7)

Activity
- Feeling Good Two (A7-8)

📄 **Resource Sheet A7-6**

Reminder: Step by Step to Responsible Assertion

These questions are helpful to use when you prepare for a situation requiring assertive behavior. However, you also have the option of using only those parts which are helpful at a particular time or in a specific situation.

- Do I want to be assertive in this situation?
- What is my objective? What exactly do I want to accomplish? (Focus on the issue in order to clarify the situation.)
- What are my rights in this situation?
- What are the rights of the other person?
- What are some of the securities I get from my usual nonassertive behavior?
- Why would I want to give them up in order to be assertive?
- Am I stopping myself from being assertive by holding on to Bad News Beliefs? How can I replace them with Good News Beliefs?
- Do I feel anxious about asserting myself? What techniques can I use to lower my anxiety?
- What do I say to:
  » Let the other person know I hear and understand her or him?
  » Let the other person know how I feel?
  » Tell her or him what I want?
- How can I evaluate my behavior? Did my nonverbal message agree with my verbal message? Did my assertion raise my self-esteem?

Resource Sheet A7-7

What Life is All About

Life isn't about keeping score. It's not about how many people call you and its not about who you've dated, are dating, or haven't dated at all. It isn't about who you kissed, what sports you play, or which guy or girl likes you. It's not about your shoes or your hair or the color of your skin or where you live or go to school. In fact, it's not about grades, money, clothes, or colleges that accept you or not. Life isn't about if you have lots of friends, or if you are alone, and its not about how accepted or unaccepted you are. Life just isn't about that.

Life is about who you love and who you hurt. It's about how you feel about yourself. It's about trust, happiness, and compassion. It's about sticking up for your friends and replacing inner hate with love. Life is about avoiding jealousy, overcoming ignorance, and building confidence. It's about seeing people for who they are and not what they have. Most of all, it is about choosing to use your life to touch someone else's in a way that could never have been achieved otherwise. These choices are what life's all about.

Pass this on to your true friends and show them how much you care about them and tell them that you love them before your life is over. —Origin Unknown

Resource Sheet A7-8

Activity: Feeling Good Two

Below are some activities you might want to do at home after the workshop is over. You might think of some other activity that would help you get a lift when you are feeling down or that has been suggested by the group.

- A giggle bulletin board with photos of yourself and friends in wild, crazy poses, photos, the best of the worst, cartoons, jokes, baby pictures, fun messages, and invitations.
- Create a peaceful place with a favorite picture, plant, objects.
- Before going to sleep, think of some of the things you accomplished that day; talked to my sister, hung up my clothes, took a long walk, did my homework, bought a flower for friend.
- Start a gratitude journal keeping track of the positive things that happen to you.

Resource Sheet A7-9

Supplemental Activity:
Setting Goals – Aftereffects Two

- Draw three pictures of your biggest problem areas below.

- Now draw three pictures of things that will lead you to happiness.

- Finally draw some pictures of what small steps you must take to get away from your problem areas to put you on the path that will lead you to happiness.
    - » Step 1: Easiest

    - » Step 2: Less easy

    - » Step 3: Even less easy

» Step 4: Most difficult

- What reward can I give myself for achieving each step?
  _____
  _____
  _____
  _____

- If I need support, who will I call? _____

Appendix B
What to Say When Problems Pop Up: Some Typical Challenges

What do you say to...

The participant who asks, "Must I be assertive?"

You are always free to choose not to assert yourself—if you are willing to put up with the consequences. Perhaps the issue or relationship is not important to you, or you may not want to take the time or there may be too much at risk. The important thing is that you make the choice so that you feel in control. You need to ask yourself, "How will I feel afterwards if I don't assert myself in this situation? However, if you find yourself deciding to be nonassertive most of the time, you will need to question your decision.

The participant who says something like, "I've always done it this other way and it works fine," or "I don't need to tell them I'm angry, they know."

That's fine. We're certainly not looking for problems if there are none. However, you may want to try your usual response with the other members of your group and then try ours. Get feedback from them on how they react. Then decide which seems better to you.

The group that has gotten off track and is gossiping or just visiting with each other.

Whose turn is it to practice?

The person who is avoiding role playing by endlessly describing the situation.

What is it you would like to say to that person? Try it on your partner.

The person who takes up too much time asking endless questions or telling endless anecdotes.

Thank you for your contribution (or question) but we need to move on (or find out what the others think).

The person whose inappropriate, sometimes bizarre remarks, questions, and actions are making the other members uncomfortable. Apparently, this person has some emotional problems or is perhaps going through an emotional crisis.

This should be said to the person in private. Tell them that assertive groups don't help everyone. I would be glad to refer you to a group that would be better for you or to a person that would talk to you individually.

The person who says, "Our church teaches us to turn the other cheek."

The Scriptures also say, "Love thy neighbor as thyself." You deserve the same sort of respect as everyone else. Christ was assertive when He threw the money changers out of the temple. In Act 16:35-40, Paul had been thrown into prison and when the authorities discovered he was a Roman citizen being held without trial, they attempted to release him without a fuss. But Paul demanded the same treatment any other Roman would have received. He demanded they come and let him out personally.

Also, when you refuse to let the other person know your appropriate feelings, opinions, or desires you are not giving that person credit for being able to handle them.

The person with conflicts about being assertive.

Try the empty-chair technique. Have the person be her nonassertive self, describing feelings and conflicts. Then have the person switch chairs allowing her assertive self to answer. Do this until the problem seems resolved.

Appendix C
Games

Change Partners
All players form pairs except one person. The player without the partner becomes the leader and gives commands for the others to follow, such as "Hand on hips," "Stand back to back," "Join right hands," "Hands on toes." Eventually the single player says "Change partners!" The player who does not get a partner becomes the leader and starts the game again.

Clap Clap
All players sit in a circle. One player (the guesser) is asked to leave the room. Select a leader who leads the clapping. She starts clapping and the player who has left comes back into the room. The leader claps her hands, then her knees, and then different parts of her body or the floor beside her. The others follow her lead but try not to look at her. When the guesser points at the leader, she leaves the room and a new leader is chosen to continue the game.

Spin the Bottle
Players sit in a circle and take turns spinning a bottle on its side in the middle of the circle. Just before spinning, the spinner asks a question, such as "Who is the best dancer in the room?" "Who is the best athlete?" "Who is the most beautiful?" The bottle answers by pointing at the player when it stops spinning.

Ha, Ha
Players sit in a circle. The first player says "ha," the next person says, "ha, ha," the third adds a ha, "ha, ha, ha," and on around the circle with each player adding another "ha." Each players must keep a straight face. Any player who laughs, smiles, or doesn't say the correct number of "ha's" is eliminated.

Who Has the Ball
One player is chosen as "it." The others stand or sit in a circle. "It" stands in the middle of the circle and closes her eyes. The other players pass a tennis ball or other object to another player who conceals it behind her. All the other players in the circle pretend they are concealing the ball also. "It" is then told to look around the circle and guess who has the ball or other object. She looks directly at that person and says "Throw me the ball (or other object)." She has three chances to guess the right person. If she fails to guess correctly another person is chosen as "it." If she guesses correctly, she changes places with the person who has the ball.

Appendix D
Suggested Agenda for a One-Day Introductory Workshop

8:30 a.m.	Complete Assertive Self-Assessment
8:40 a.m.	Skill: Assertive Introductions
8:50 a.m.	Explanation of Purpose of Workshop
9:00 a.m.	Distinguishing differences among aggressive, assertive, and nonassertive behavior
9:30 a.m.	Respecting Rights Rights Swap Meet

10:15 a.m.	Identifying personal blocks to assertion and diminishing them.
	   Bad News Beliefs (Irrational Beliefs)
	   Good News Beliefs

11:00 a.m.	Skill: Reading Body Language
11:30 a.m.	Giving and Receiving Compliments
12:00 noon	Lunch

1:00 p.m.	Learning to Say "No"
	   Handling Peer Pressure
	     Skill: Persistence (Broken Record)
	     Skill: Role Playing Saying "No"

2:00 p.m.	Admitting Mistakes, Handling Criticism, Expressing Feelings Name that Feeling Skill: Admitting Mistakes Skill: Handling Put-downs (Criticism) Skill: "I" Language (Expressing Feelings and Needs)
3:00 p.m.	Social Skill: Conversations
3:20 p.m.	The Link
3:25 p.m.	You're Awesome!

Appendix E
Glossary

aggressive behavior. Standing up for one's rights and expressing one's thoughts, feelings, and beliefs in a way that is dishonest, usually inappropriate, and violates the rights of the other person. The goal is domination or winning by humiliating, degrading, belittling, insulting, or overpowering another person.

assertive behavior. Being able to express one's feeling, make free choices, and meet more of one's personal needs without experiencing undue guilt or anxiety and without violating the rights and dignity of others.

broken record/persistence. A technique in which one repeats what one wants over and over again without getting angry, loud, or irritated. Can be used with manipulative, aggressive persons so as to be heard and to keep from being drawn into side issues.

comfort level. A scale of zero to 100 measuring one's level of anxiety.

defensive. Responses that seek to protect one against perceived attack by being resistant and offering excuses, alibis, rationalizations, reasons, and justifications.

desensitize: Make less irritating, painful, or uncomfortable.

discrimination test. Used to test the understanding of the differences in behavior.

empathy. Compassion and understanding in which one knows what the other person is feeling by imagining themselves in the same situation.

expanded opinion: Expressing one's opinion with one explanation.

feedback. Any kind of return information that is useful in modifying behavior.

fogging. A nondefensive technique to protect oneself from manipulative criticism in which one puts psychological distance between oneself and the criticizer. It is a passive rather than an assertive skill and should only be used as a last resort, to shut off further arguments.

hidden rehearsal. The process of imagining oneself responding successfully, or as one would like to, in a particular situation.

modeling. Demonstrating for observers a behavior the observers wish to learn.

nonassertive behavior. (1) Violating your rights by either failing to express your honest feelings, thoughts, and beliefs, and consequently permitting others to take advantage of you, or (2) expressing your thoughts, beliefs, and feelings in such an apologetic, cautious, and unconfident manner that other people disregard them.

passive-aggressive. Initially meek, mild behavior used to manipulate with guilt, or punish the other person.

peer. Persons of one's own age group.

role play. Acting out a situation in which one plays a role or practices behavior that one would like to use in a similar, real-life situation.

secondary gain. Special treatment from others when one acts weak and nonassertive.

self-assessment. A self-measurement instrument to measure assertive behavior before and after training. This instrument provides information on the areas in which trainees may want to improve their skills and the progress they have made.

self-esteem, self-concept. One's evaluation of one's self.

self-disclosure. Behavior or speech that reveals the thoughts and feelings of the person.

thought stoppage. The technique of controlling unwanted thoughts by using the word "stop" at first shouted aloud and eventually said silently to oneself.

toxic waste/shame. Thoughts that can poison your belief in yourself so that you are unable to act effectively thereby lowering your self-esteem.

workable compromise. An alternate way of doing things that both parties accept. Negotiating an acceptable solution.

Appendix F
Journal Sheet of Assertive Behavior*

Date	Behavior	Person	Satisfactory Aspects of Performance	Needs Improvement	Overall: Excellent, Good, Fair, Poor; Level of Comfort	My Behavior: Aggressive, Nonassertive, Assertive, Passive/Aggressive
Sample						
1/5	refused request	friend	eye contact	sarcastic	poor; level 90	aggressive

*Adapted with permission from *Assert Yourself! How to Be Your Own Person*, by Merna Dee Galassi and John Galassi. New York: Human Services Press/Kluwer Publishers, 1977.

Appendix G
Resources and Recommended Readings

Branden, N. *Psychology of Self-Esteem.* San Francisco: Jossey-Bass, 2000.

Carter, William, Lee. *The Angry Teenager.* Nashville: Thomas Nelson, Inc., 1995.

Clark, Aminair, Harris Clemes, and Reynold Beam. *How to Raise Teenagers' Self-Esteem,* Los Angeles: Price, Stern, and Sloan, 1990.

Corey, Gerald. *Theory and Practice of Group Counseling,* 5th ed. Pacific Grove, Calif.: Brooks/Cole Publishing, 2000.

Egan, G. *Exercises in Helping Skills: A Training Manual to Accompany the Skilled Helper.* Monterey, Calif.: Brooks/Cole Publishing Company, 1990.

Ellis, Albert, and R. A. Harper. *A New Guide to Rational Living.* Englewood Cliffs, N.J.: Prentice-Hall, 1978.

Galassi, Merna Dee, and John P. Galassi. *Assert Yourself!* New York: Human Sciences Press, 1977.

Glendlin, Eugene. *Focusing.* New York: Bantam Books, 1982.

Khalsa, SiriNam S. *Group Exercises for Enhancing Social Skill and Self-Esteem.* Sarasota, Fla.: Professional Resource Press, 1999.

Mackay, Matthew, and Patrick Fanning. *Self-Esteem.* Oakland, Calif.: New Harbinger Publications, 1992.

Manis, Laura G. *Assertion Training Workshop,* Rev. ed. Holmes Beach, Fla.: Learning Publications, 1998.

Mihaly, Mary E. *Getting Your Own Way.* New York: M. Evans and Company, 1979.

Reasoner, R. "What's Behind Self-Esteem Programs: Truth or Trickery?" *The School Executive* 1 (April 1992): 1-20.

Simon, Toby, and Cathy A. Harris. *Sex Without Consent.* Holmes Beach, Fla.: Learning Publications, Inc., 1996.

Simon, Sidney B., Leland W. Howe, and Howard Kirschenbaum. *Values Clarification.* New York: Hart Publishing Inc., 1995.

Yalom, I. D. *The Theory and Practice of Group Psychotherapy.* New York: Basic Books, 1985.

Recommended Readings

Arredia, Joni. *Sex, Boys, and You: Be Your Own Best Friend.* Toledo, Ohio: Perc Publishing, 1998.

Booher, Dianna Daniels. *Making Friends with Yourself and Other Strangers.* New York, Julian Messner, 1982.

Dee, Catherine. *The Girls Guide to Life.* Canada: Little, Brown, and Company, 1997.

Covey, Sean. *The Seven Habits of Highly Effective Teens.* New York: Simon and Schuster, 1998.

Fishel, Danielle. *Girls Get Real.* New York: Scholastic Trade, 1999.

Havelin, Kate. *Assertiveness: How Can I Say What I Mean?* Mankato, Minn.: Capstone Press, 2000.

Johnston, Andrea. *Girls Speak Out: Finding Your True Self.* New York: Scholastic Press, 1997.

Pipher, Mary. *Reviving Ophelia: Saving the Selves of Adolescent Girls.* New York: Balantine Books, 1995.

Schneider, Meg F. *Popularity Has Its Ups and Downs.* New York: Julian Messner, 1991.

Schwager, Tina, and Michele Schueger. *Gutsy Girls; Young Women Who Dare.* Minneapolis, Minn.: Free Spirit Publishing, 1999.